MY LIFE

JUST DO IT!

Volume One

1933-1962

RON DAMRILL

ISBN: 9798340228383

My Life

ACKNOWLEDGMENTS

I wish to thank all who have inspired me to devote the time to finally placing into writing the many experiences I have enjoyed in my life. Especially my devoted wife Lynda who spent many hours proofing my drafts. Then there is a special recognition for the four members of my Authors Critique Group in The Villages Florida. Through our scheduled meetings I have grown my knowledge of being an author, and have been inspired to make this possible.

Thanks, Larry, Tom, Dick, and Ron.

TABLE OF CONTENTS

Chapter 1. 1
Chapter 2 7
Chapter 4. 19
Chapter 5. 27
Chapter 6. 33
Chapter 7. 40
Chapter 8. 46
Chapter 9. 52
Chapter 10. 59
Chapter 11. 65
Chapter 12. 71
Chapter 13. 78
Chapter 14. 85
Chapter 15. 91
Chapter 16. 99
Chapter 17. 106
Chapter 18. 114
Chapter 19. 122
Chapter 20. 130
Chapter 21.1 137
Chapter 21.2 145
Chapter 22. 151
Chapter 23. 158

Chapter 24. 165
Chapter 25. 172
Chapter 26. 179
Chapter 27. 187
Chapter 28. 194
Chapter 29. 202
Chapter 30. 209
Chapter 31 216
Chapter 32 222
Chapter 33 229
Chapter 34 236
Chapter 35 243
Chapter 36 250

CHAPTER 1.

Time to write a biography. How to do it, the media and Hollywood seem to suggest that you can't be a success unless you have had a personal disaster or disability. If you haven't had such a happening, then persons in your ancestry must have been poor or had to have had a disaster. Even if you must go back as far as the Pilgrims Landing or Adam and Eve. On second thought maybe the media is trying to say that In the United States, you can succeed no matter your personal situation or background. Accordingly, I'll start with some family events. I don't consider them a disaster. I consider them as challenges, colorful events, and great adventures.

My mother's father emigrated from Sweden in the 1900's. They first went to Minnesota. He got a mining job as an immigrant. Then watched and realized that the people who handle dynamite (blasters) were paid more money. So, he got hired in the dynamite crew. He was offered a dynamite job at Minden Mines, Missouri. About 10 miles from Pittsburg, Kansas. There was a lot of coal mining in that area. He continued working in dynamiting and was successful for several years. If you set an explosion and the fuse fizzled, you had to return to the dynamite charge and take out the old fuse. He did that. His luck ran out and this time the fuse relighted before he could take it out and he was blown up, but not killed. After a year he fully recovered and returned to his old job. Again, the fuse fizzled, and he had to replace it. But the fuse relit and blew him up again. This time he was blinded for life. This was about 1926. My maternal grandmother died from cancer in her early 40s. My mom two brothers and a sister were still at home.

There was a widow nearby with several children and no income. I believe my grandfather was getting a pension from the accident. She agreed to marry him and take care of him provided her children could come with her. She undertook a demanding job taking care of a person who was blind. With his children and her children, there were too many. This created a financial problem. Not enough money. My grandfather's teenage kids decided they should go on their own. My mother was determined to finish high school, which few did in those days. Twenty-two percent completed high school in 1928. To accomplish this task, she became a live-in housemaid in Pittsburg, Kansas. She continued to college and completed one semester. Then the stock market crashed in 1929 followed by the "Great Depression." She quit college and got a job as a secretary at the local airfield. A short time later she got married.

My dad was born in 1908. He finished the eighth grade. In 1932 my dad was grinding on a piece of metal and got a piece of steel in his eye. He lost his eye. He was not wearing goggles. My dad was a heavy smoker and coupled with that he started a business that created a lot of smoke that he breathed. Consequently, he died of a heart attack at 42 in 1950.

My mom had living with her had me who had just graduated high school at age 17, my sister was 13, and her sister and her child age 4. She received money from a small life insurance policy. She had very little money. My mom got a job working for a local candy vending machine company at $40 a week. As the Korean War continued, they opened an ammunition plant in Parson, Kansas and she got a higher-paying job. She was also able to receive child support from Social Security.

I started my first semester at college and to pay my way I rode my motor scooter delivering telegrams for Western Union. College was inexpensive. For $60, that paid for the semester, and they loaned you the books at no cost. The Korean War had started in the summer and was continuing. At the end of the semester, I turned 18 in January 1951, and I joined the Marine Corps.

One of my mom's brothers was having a tough time when the Depression hit in 1929 and was having difficulty getting a job. So, like many people his age during the Depression they took to being a hobo and sneaking rides on freight cars. He got into a confrontation with a security guard and accidentally fell under a moving train and had his arm cut off.

My mom's other brother became a railroad engineer, and her sister married a carpenter.

On Lynda's side of the family. Lynda's mom's first husband and her two young children died of tuberculosis. Her Mom's second husband was Lynda's dad, and they had Lynda who turned out perfect. Lynda's dad died about 62 years old of lung complications from working in the coal mines in Tennessee at a young age. It was 1969. Lynda had a younger sister born with leg and arm disabilities coupled with a weak heart and lungs. She died at about the age of 42.

My wife Lynda's great-grandfathers and my great-great-grandfather both fought in the Civil War. Lynda's great-grandfather starved to death as a prisoner in the Southern "Prisoner of War" camp at Andersonville. His name was George Washington Pennington.

My grandfather (actually my step-grandfather) was an artilleryman in World War I and fought several artillery duels with the Germans. I forgot to mention that my grandfather on my dad's side was a half-breed Indian (Cherokee). In 1890, in Oklahoma, it was a hostile environment for a half-breed Indian. He became a wanderer. Perhaps looking for the "Happy Hunting Ground." He had met and married my grandmother in 1906. My dad was born in 1908. In 1912 they moved to Idaho. My grandmother had another boy and a girl. They both died within a year of birth. She had had enough of the tragedy in Idaho and told my grandfather, Will Damrill, that she wanted to go back to Pittsburg, Kansas. He refused to return. My grandmother was determined. She packed up and with my dad returned to Pittsburg,

Kansas in 1916. She met and married my step-granddad shortly after he returned from France and WW I in 1919.

I finally met my granddad one time in Chicago when I was 10 in 1943. He was about 55. The meeting was cordial. But lacked enthusiasm. At that time, he was married to a girl who appeared to be about 29. She was very attractive. There were two other small children present. Don't know if they were his. He had an interesting life. He had been a private detective and numerous other jobs. Now he was working in law enforcement.

I think I have come up with enough of life's challenges and adventures to make us successful with the liberal media. They would consider this tearful, but we considered it a colorful events in the family history.

I was born on 25 January 1933. In the back bedroom of the house on 311 E. Quincy in Pittsburg, Kansas. No hospital. Not sure if a doctor was present.

Unknown at the time. I was born with a heredity eye problem known as BEST (adult-onset vermicular vitelliform dystrophy). I am not sure if it could be identified at that time based on medical progress in 1933. About 1% of the people in Sweden have this as an inherited problem. It feels like the optic nerve is being squeezed. Making the eye images fight through to the optic nerve to get to the brain. Like blood trying to get through a blocked artery to get to the heart.

I did not know I had BEST until it was diagnosed at the age of 55. It is a good thing because today if it is identified you will not be permitted to serve in the military. It is a medical disqualification. In WW II terms you were "4F."

Below I will try to explain how BEST vision affected me physically.

I see things as an overview, but seeing the detail is the problem. For example, I can see the page of a book, but to pick out specific words requires an extreme amount of focus. It was almost point-and-read. Consequently, reading was a very slow process. I could read maybe 10 pages of a textbook in one hour. Subconsciously I would start to spot read filling in the spaces with what I thought the author was going to say. Many times, I would misinterpret the meaning. I was always last to complete a test. Fortunately, I was able to complete it in time. In the early years of education teachers would require students to read aloud. For me that was impossible.

At age 17, a freshman in college, the BEST really hit hard. My eyes felt like they were looking through binoculars that were out of focus. The stress of trying to constantly refocus and transmit images to the brain was exhausting. It was extremely difficult to read the blackboard. I would have to read a textbook one word at a time and my eyes became so focused on the text that when I completed reading my refocus on seeing distant objects took several hours. This condition lasted for five years until I was age 22. At 22 the condition reduced itself overnight to 80%, just in time for me to enroll in advanced ROTC (Junior & Senior). Prior military service gave you credit for the first two years. However, I still had the same reading problems but the focus stress on the eyes was reduced by 80%.

I certainly was confused about my ability.

Here I am. Haven't even started. All washed up. Who believed that in a few years, I would be meeting with United States Ambassadors in foreign lands.

At age 45 I discovered an additional problem. My wife was a counselor, and she was testing children on their hearing ability. The test's basic idea was can you hear someone talking when there is noise in the background. My wife gave me the test and to her surprise, I scored the lowest of all those tested. In other words, if I heard background noise that canceled all noise out, so I heard nothing. The result is usually I heard only 80 to 90% of what was being said in the classroom or at staff meetings. To test myself I recorded a meeting and played back and was surprised how much I had missed and how it altered what I had understood, during the meeting. I had noticed previously when I was in a military operation center, with several radios on at the same time, I only heard noise all the radios canceling themselves out. I was amazed at the time some people could hear two or three radios at the same time. I had to put the earphones next to my ear to hear the transmission. The test explained to me why I had difficulty hearing conversations in noisy areas.

Reflecting during college and trying to listen to the professor while he simultaneously wrote on a blackboard. Not only could I not see because the professor's body was in front of the words written on the blackboard. And t I only heard a portion of what he was saying and being further detracted by trying to take notes. I'm surprised I got through college at all. I did end up in the upper half of the class's academic standing. In military classes, it was much easier. They lectured using numerous training aids versus only the blackboard. In the military they would tell you, show you and you may have a tactical exercise to reinforce the show and tell. Additionally, they would give you a summary sheet at the end of the classes outlining the key points you should have learned. This allowed the student to concentrate on what was being taught and not have to try to write at the same time. In most military classes I finished in the top 10%.

Growing up, it's good that I was unaware of my shortcomings. Since these shortcomings can be easily identified in today's environment, I'm sure they would convince me at age 6 that I was the victim and should be on welfare as an unproductive citizen.

To top this off my mother enrolled me in the first grade at 5 years old. We fibbed to the administration that I was six years old. You could do that in 1938. She thought it was good for me to finish school a year early to get a jumpstart. Being one to two years younger than my classmates was interesting. You might say I was a little immature, at times, compared to other boys in the class. And it made a difference in sports. However, at the time I didn't notice. It was in later years watching children grow up that I noticed the difference.

CHAPTER 2

A little more on family background. My Mom played basketball in high school at Minden Mines., Missouri.

My step-granddad on my dad's side was solid and I don't think he got much credit for it at the time. He was in the artillery during World War I and fought several artillery duels with the German artillery. He worked for the WPA during the Depression. Later he took a good position with a coal company as a steam shovel operator. The company had great confidence in him by letting him operate their primary piece of equipment. At that time in Pittsburgh Kansas, they were doing strip coal mining. The coal was maybe 50 feet below the surface, and they shoveled the dirt from the top to get to it. Because it was a lucrative job he provided the financial base for the family during the 30s, 40s, and 50s. He had one son who joined the Navy in WW II and married his buddy's sister in Cleveland Ohio. He later became a newspaper distributor. He continued to live in Cleveland Ohio. He was divorced after they had a couple of children. They remained friends.

In 1939 my dad started his own business making optical supplies. During the start-up period, he continued his downtown job. This company made a tar or glue-like substance which was used to hold the glass on a tool while the glass was ground to the desired prescription. The company sold other items used in the optical business. His product was sold to the company responsible for the optical lenses for the Norton bomb sight during WW II. This was a breakthrough invention that provided bombers with greater accuracy in hitting targets

By 1941 he was having success in his business and he quit his downtown job. Going into business was a great risk if you had a family to support. No steady paycheck. You stood alone. You had to have strong confidence your idea would succeed. Having achieved a degree of success allowed the family to move to a middle-income neighborhood in the Belmont district of Dayton. The house was on Spring Mount Avenue. My dad set up his business location about four blocks from the house. There was gas rationing and being close to home saved on gas. You were allocated 4 gallons a week.

Starting in the sixth grade at about 10 years old I began working after school for my dad building plywood trays used in the optical business. They were about 8" x 12" and 1 inch high. I did this job until the end of the eighth grade. I was paid by the number of boxes produced. I averaged 50 cents per hour. Good money for the time. During this period school really seemed to be boring. Maybe the age factor was catching up. Of course that is the beginning of the preteen years.

While on Chaple Street from 1938-1942 I remember going to the river and going out as far as possible on the ice. You kept going until you heard the ice start to crack. A challenge to see how far you could go. In the summertime, we swam in the same polluted river and waded across neck high in water. No one could swim. They dredged gravel for the bottom of the river, and we would go jump off the pile and slide down the hill. At the bottom were pools of water and we would stop short of slipping into the water. One student didn't stop in time and drowned.

I remember in the fourth grade my first girlfriend's name was Roberta Wampler. Of course, I never talked to her. In the seventh grade I remember another girl named Geraldine Long and I never talked to her. Too shy. I'm surprised I remember the names.

In the 5th through 8th grade, I wasn't connected socially to the desired level. I had come from a small school where I was a VIP. Now I was the new kid on the block in a large school. My mom was busy with business and no longer interested in the PTA. I was discouraged by my popularity in junior high.

I had been to Sunday School and heard about prayer. To me, prayer seemed vague. I was extremely frustrated in the 6th grade, and I decided to try a prayer. I was standing in the playground and said a prayer for assistance, I requested having the popularity status of an average student. Just average. Much to my surprise I felt a response. The heavens seemed to open, and I felt what seemed like a warm beam embracing me. It all happened in a second and I wasn't sure what to think about it. It was like acknowledging that my message was received. I am not particularly religious, so I was surprised. Nothing happened immediately. But slowly things begin to improve. In high school things happened beyond belief.

1942 – My new middle-class neighborhood spread out with a lower density of children to play with. I noticed when you moved to a new neighborhood where everyone knew each other from 1st grade it was hard to break in socially.

Some of my adventures on Springmount Avenue were to break my arm, get my first dog, and make a rabbit trap that I put in the backyard. Caught one rabbit, but didn't know what to do with it. So, I let it go. Also, had a BB gun and attempted to shoot the neighborhood birds. After several months of trying and several hundred BB's, I finally hit one. The feathers flew. I thought I was now in the class of the "Great White Hunters in Africa." Before I finished that thought the bird flew away uninjured. The event reminded me of my dad's hero "Frank Buck." In the 20's and 30's Frank Buck was a big game hunter, adventurer, and eventually a movie star. My dad would have liked to follow Frank Buck's lifestyle. Unfortunately, he didn't listen closely to the lyrics of the song "Don't Fence Me In." Instead, he got married and became domesticated. That ended the hope of being another Frank Buck.

1943 -The sixth-grade homeroom class was very unruly. When the teacher's back was turned everyone threw spitballs at each other and other paper obstacles. As a result, the boys were put on trial by the ninth-grade civics class. Of course, I was innocent, but found guilty, and sentenced to sweep out the school hallways and auditorium after school for one month. All the boys were found guilty. I was age 10 - 11 years old. We had a poor defense attorney. Today you would call it gender prejudice.

In 1944 we had assemblies once a week and would have a guest speaker. One event featured a Communist. I remember the end of his speech saying. "At the end of the war reach your hand across the seas to grasp Joe Stalin's hand and say let's go Joe." I thought of a strange thing to say. But we were sort of allies at the time.

In eighth-grade shop class, I must have done something wrong because the teacher called me to the front of the class and had me bend over for a paddling. I thought that it would be insignificant. However, I found that the wooden paddle used had a significant sting associated with it. I thought paddling in those days was very effective as was the previous trial of the civics class.

I thought downtown Dayton was a long way. Recently visited Dayton. Downtown was not as far as I remembered at age 11. For example, the distance downtown was only 3 miles. During World War II. I would ride the bus to various events downtown such as movies or the Art Institute. The buses were always crowded because of the gas rationing and stopped at almost every corner. The cost was three cents. And as you rode along you could see the different colored stars displayed in the windows of the houses. This meant that a member of the household was serving military or had been killed in the military. If there was a gold Star it meant that a member of the household had been killed.

The 4th of July was great. I would buy large firecrackers and put them under tin cans to see how high I could blow them.

In 1944 I would go to a park that belonged to the National Cash Register Company. You had to find someone who worked there and have them loan you their pass to get in. I remember going to Wright-Patterson Airfield. I was 12 years old and would ride my bike from home. The distance was 3-4 miles. I would park at the end of the runway and watch the planes fly as they landed. When they had an airshow I would ride the bus. At one airshow they had a hospital tent set up for demonstration and included several soldiers who had been wounded in combat. You could see their wounds. They also had parachutes for airborne demonstrations. On one occasion I saw a paratrooper whose chute didn't open. He crashed into the ground and was killed. He could not get his reserve parachute to work. At another show an experimental aircraft (XP-55) zoomed over the crowd and went out of control, crashing into cars parked along the edge of the airfield. The crash created a gigantic ball of fire killing several.

My dad bought an inboard motorboat, and we went to Indian Lake on several occasions.

1944 - On Springmont Avenue, I was in my bedroom on the second story when I heard a loud roar – with windows shaking and shortly thereafter followed by a loud boom. A pilot had lost control of his P-47 fighter but managed to direct it out of the neighborhood and crashed three blocks away in an open field. The pilot had stayed with the airplane and was killed. I went to the crash site and retrieved a small piece of the wreckage before the crash site was secured by the military.

1944 Gene Autry came to town at the local theater. It was summer so I went to the theater to see him. I thought the theater would be packed and it would be tough getting in. But I was surprised the theater was only half full. I thought about how this could be when he was so popular as a singer and cowboy star at the time. Just an observation.

1945 -World War II came to an end while living on Springmont Avenue. We went to downtown Dayton to celebrate the victory. The crowd was enormous.

1946 -- moved to an upper-income neighborhood in the "Upper Dayton View" district of Dayton. Only half a block from the junior high school. It was Col. White Junior High School. Attended the ninth grade and it was a super school. But the neighborhood kids were really spread out. Hard to make friends as a new person. At age 13 I saw my first polio victim. She survived but had one leg smaller than the other.

1946 – My dad attempted to expand his business during this period. He decided to go into the lens-grinding business. Lens which were used for

eyeglasses. This is where you grind prescriptions into the glasses that people will later wear. You get a glass blank which is a molded piece of glass and attach it to a tool with glue/tar-like. The glue/tar substance is what my dad manufactured in his first business. Once attached it is ground and polished to the prescription specified by the optometrist. To remove the glass from the tool, dip it in cold water. I spent the summer between the eighth and ninth-grade grinding glasses. This setup took a lot of floor space and equipment. Unfortunately, my dad could not compete with the larger companies.

He had sold his previous business to returning soldiers who wanted to go into business.

With the second business being unprofitable we decided to go back to Pittsburgh Kansas.

1947 – I was delighted to leave Dayton Ohio. I thought everything was overregulated at age 14. Going to Pittsburgh Kansas was freedom. I had just gotten a motor scooter before leaving Dayton. In Kansas, you could get a driver's license at age 14. All I needed was one dollar and I was on the open road. The good thing about small towns, it is difficult to get into trouble and you have freedom.

CHAPTER 3

The 4th of July was great. I would buy large firecrackers and put them under tin cans to see how high I could blow them. Being large they created a lot of noise. All the boys in the neighborhood kept the noise going blowing up anything they could find. Neighbors enjoyed the fun and noise. No one complained or came running out scolding kids that they might blow off their fingers. Boys climbed trees, and rode bicycles everywhere exploring and doing all the things of interest to boys. Parents and neighbors encouraged boys to be boys.

Business was good and my dad bought a boat. It was an 18-foot Mullin Inboard Aluminum Boat. There was a lake a few miles away where we spent several weekends and one summer spent an entire week in a cabin. My first experience living on a lake. It was great. Almost got my dad interested in buying an airplane. But, he had only one eye and thought that may cause a problem. I mentioned he had lost his eye when grinding a piece of steel in 1932. The story was that he was under consideration for draft even with one eye. His duty would have been in the optical field. Having a business that supported the war effort gave him a deferment.

During the summers I made frequent trips to a park that belonged to the National Cash Register Company. You had to find someone who worked there and have them loan you their pass to get in.

When employees were caught, they were given a slight reprimand by management.

Summertime was great for airshows at Wright-Patterson Field. I was 12 years old and would ride my bike from home to the airshow. About four miles. At one airshow they had a field hospital tent with real wounded soldiers direct from the battlefield. The wounds shown were very large. Much more devastating than those shown in the movies. Another demonstration was parachute troops jumping from planes at an altitude of 1000 feet. As they passed all parachutes opened. Except one. The paratrooper's chute failed and became twisted. Called a Roman candle. He tried to get to his reserve parachute. But too late. He was hit with a thump and was killed. Doesn't take long to fall 1,00 feet. Estimate 15 seconds or less. Depends on the drag of the unopened parachute.

At another show, an experimental fighter aircraft (XP-55) zoomed over the crowd doing a half-barrel roll and went out of control crashing into cars parked at the end of the runway. Several killed. Lot of casualties at these airshows. When there wasn't an airshow I would ride my bicycle to Wright-Paterson and sit outside the fence at the end of the runway and watch planes land.

1944 - On Spring Mont Avenue, I was in my bedroom on the second story, one afternoon, when I heard a loud roar. The windows shook. Then a loud boom shook every object in the house. Felt like an earthquake. A pilot had lost control of his P-47 fighter but managed to direct it out of the neighborhood and crashed two blocks away in an open field. The pilot had stayed with the fighter and was killed. I rushed to the crash site and arrived before security was established. The fighter had made a large hole in the ground and there was wreckage everywhere. I quickly picked up a small piece of aluminum wreckage and headed for home as security arrived. A real treasure had been obtained.

1945 Gene Autry and his horse came to downtown Dayton at the local theater. It was summer and decided to take part in the event. Expected the theater to be packed and be tough getting in. But the theater was only half full. How could this be when he was so popular as a singer, cowboy, and movie star? This was the first time seeing a real movie star.

World War II came to an end on August 14, 1945, with the surrender of Japan. The family decided to go to downtown Dayton to celebrate. The crowd was enormous. The streets were packed, stopping all traffic. The celebration went on for hours. A lifetime event.

1946 -- moved to the upper-income neighborhood in "Upper Dayton View" district of Dayton. Only a half block from the junior high school. The name was Col. White Junior High School and a super school. Attended the ninth grade. But the neighbor kids were few and spread out. New kid on the block. At age 13 I saw my first polio victim. She survived but had one leg that looked like a stick and was smaller around than the other.

My dad was attempting to expand his business activities and get into a more profitable part of the optical field. He sold his old business and decided to go into lens grinding. This is where you start with a blank piece of round glass and grind it to the desired prescriptions as ordered by the optometrist. To start the process, you take a raw piece of round glass and attach it to a tool with glue-tar-like substance. This substance is what my dad manufactured in his first business. Once attached it is ground and polished to the prescription. To remove the glass from the tool it is dipped it in cold water. I spent the summer between the eighth and ninth-grade grinding glasses. Unfortunately, my dad could not compete with the larger established companies. Having failed in this business he decided to move back to Pittsburg, Kansas.

1947 – I was delighted to leave Dayton Ohio. I thought everything was overregulated at age 14. Going to Pittsburgh Kansas was freedom. I had just gotten a motor scooter before leaving Dayton.

In Kansas, you could get a driver's license at age 14. All that was needed was one dollar and you were on the open road. The good thing about a small town, it is difficult to get into trouble and you have freedom.

1947 -Upon arriving in Pittsburg, Kansas I had six weeks of school left. In algebra, I got credit for being super bright in this subject. Dayton was 6 months ahead of Pittsburg in math. And their math teacher was letting students read comic books in class. The teacher was later fired.

I even joined the 4th of July parade with my decorated motor scooter. This was with the encouragement of my mom who decorated the scooter. Won first prize among decorated scooters. Boys my age with scooters hung out at the Cushman motorscooter dealer. That was a great lazy summer. Hanging out and exploring the open road.

By hanging out at the Cushman dealership It was learned you could make money with your scooter by delivering packages for the drug store. WOW, paid to explore the city. What more could be asked?

A few days later I got a job at a Drug Store and started delivering medical prescriptions.

Exploring ways to make money it was discovered you could get paid for delivering new phone books door to door. I volunteered for the job and was accepted. Felt like a postman. You got 2 or 3 cents for each telephone book delivered and another 2 or 3 cents if you could get the customer to surrender the old book. One hot afternoon, while making deliveries, got very thirsty and saw a tavern. Had been in taverns with my uncle so thought it was all right to go in. Didn't know about the age requirement. I walked into the tavern and seated myself at the bar. There was a black bartender, and he had an astonished look on his face. I thought that was strange. I ordered an orange soda. When he came back with the soda he had a large smile of amusement on his face, Again, couldn't figure out what this was about. Then looked around the tavern and all the customers were black. All smiling in amusement. This was my first experience in an all-black tavern. As I drank the soda, they were watching my every move in amusement. I finished the soda and left.

I'm sure I was the tavern's entertainment that afternoon. An underage white boy enters a black tavern and orders a soda. And it was obvious the kid had no idea what he was doing or what was happening.

In Pittsburgh Kansas at the age of 14, I discovered that the YMCA had a 22-caliber shooting range on the top floor. I remember grabbing my rifle and a couple of boxes of ammunition going to the top floor and using the YMCA range for target practice. Not sure there was supervision. Believe you were trusted to do the right thing.

1947 -1948 Reference weapons. In high school, we would go duck hunting in the morning and come straight to high school and put our shotgun into our wall locker. You could bring pistols to school, use blanks, and fire them on stage during Western plays. Most kids felt if they did something really dumb or criminal that their future lives would be finished. No second chance. Finished.

CHAPTER 4.

1947 - Starting high school as a new guy in a small town, where everyone had been going to school together since kindergarten, it was tough trying to be one of the groups. Felt out of place and like a misfit. But, after the first semester, things got good. For some reason, a popular guy and his girlfriend decided to adopt me and be my mentor. They were in the popular working-class group. Not from the wealthy society in-group. The so-called in-group was envied because they had stylish clothes, money, and good cars. At the end of my sophomore year, I was riding high. In the Junior and senior years, the above girl and boy became cheerleaders, and she was elected Prom Queen her senior year.

Only saw one case of discipline during my three years in high school. On the first day of school, in a typing class, there was a wise guy determined to disrupt the class. The teacher was a big guy who was a reserve Captain in the Marine Corps. He didn't say a word to the student. Just walked over to the student's desk, picked him up two feet, and dropped him. Falling two feet hurt. Never heard a peep from the student again.

1948 -That summer, at age 15, I decided to go to the Civil Air Patrol camp at the Air Force base near Omaha, Nebraska. I and other cadets were picked up in Joplin, Missouri, and flown in a B-17 World War II bomber. During the flight, they placed me in the bombardier's seat in the nose of the aircraft. This position provided the opportunity to simulate bombing targets all the way to Omaha. The two-week summer camp sponsored by the Air Force was well organized. They provided uniforms, flying lessons, mess hall dining, and tents to sleep in. The weather was sunny every day. During one day of training at the airfield, witnessed an airplane landing with one engine on fire. On other days pilots took cadets on flights and allowed them to fly. A couple of planes used were a T-6 trainer and a C-47 transport. The C-47 was the plane paratroopers jumped from on D-Day. At the end of camp, we were flown home in the C-47. During the flight, cadets were allowed to practice flying for a few minutes from the co-pilot seat.

The rest of the summer worked with my dad and uncle renovating used cars. If I wasn't working, my mom made sure I had an allowance of $5 a week. Today, with inflation, that $5 would be about $80. She was determined that High School would be a special event.

1948 – This was my junior year, and my parents had bought me an old used car. When it broke, they let me take the family car, in the evening. At age 15, this High School period was outstanding. Socialized all day on campus and out every night on the town. Not many had a car and those wanting to join me in an adventure jumped in. However, Pittsburg, Kansas was a slow and quiet town and it took creative thinking to find new adventures.

I had a good time. Participating in all evening school activities gave me great visibility and recognition. Being highly motivated, with recent success, took a chance, and signed up for the Junior School Play. Passed the audition and was in the play. My character wasn't the lead but, it had the most lines and stage time. This was beyond my expectations.

1949 - That summer, at age 16, signed up for the Civil Air Patrol Camp at an Air Force base in Oklahoma. One of the cadets' fathers had a private airplane and flew me and his son to Oklahoma. At this camp, sponsors didn't seem as motivated as those in the previous year. We were billeted in a WW II style barracks. Their training program was flat and lacked excitement and adventure. The only adventure I recall was that the Colonel's daughter walked by the barracks and some of the cadets whistled at her. I suspect she walked by on purpose. The Air Force officer, responsible for the cadets, was reprimanded. It then became necessary for him to reprimand a cadet. Someone had to pay. This was interesting and just like a WW II fiction military movie. The next thing I knew I was being called in as the culprit. Someone said they saw me nearby. This was my first experience being set up. Should have demanded to see the person who made the allegation. The accuser was probably the guilty party. The whole thing seemed to be exaggerated. The takeaway from the story is to blame someone else if you're guilty. Anyway, stuck with no alibi. My punishment was to march up and down the parade field for two hours with a rifle on my shoulder. They should have required me to apologize in person. That way would get to see the girl. Always demand to see your accuser. On the upside, it made me very popular with the other cadets. I didn't tell on the others who were involved. Of course, I couldn't, because I didn't know. A hero anyway.

Returning home, found a farmer who wanted help bailing hay and needed four more farm hands. Return to Pittsburg and recruited four classmates. They were city boys and scoffed at the idea of being a farmhand. After a short discussion, it dawned on them that they were unemployed, and this was a job offer. We loaded up in a car and took to the field. In 1949 hay bailers were very crude and lacked automation and a lot of the work was done by hand in a cloud of swirling dust. The bailer scooped up the cut hay from the ground, compressed it into bails, and sent it down a conveyor-type chute. As these bails were pushed down the chute, they had to be secured by wrapping two pieces of wire around them to hold their shape. This was started by placing a wooden block, built with slots to pass wires through, in front of a new bail to keep one end compressed as it passed down the conveyer belt. When the bail was full size another block was placed behind. Then two wires had to be passed by a worker on one side to another worker on the other side who tied the wires before the bail was pushed out of the chute. A trailer was towed behind and as the bales came out they were grabbed by another farm hand, with a hook in hand, and placed on the trailer. When the trailer was fully loaded, they were transferred to a truck. Bails were stacked about six high and not tied down. When the truck was loaded, we climbed on top and rode to the barn. If the truck happened to swerve around a corner, with these unsecured bails, we and the bails would have come tumbling down.

Enroute to the barn we passed through a small town of three thousand people and saw them moving a two-story house on roller-type wheels. One of the employees was supervising the move from on top and didn't notice electric wires hanging across the road. He hit them and was either electrocuted or knocked from the roof. It was fatal. They were carrying him away dead. After that adventure, we finally arrived at the barn and unloaded the truck by stacking the bales into the hay loft of the barn.

We all had a great time and it's surprising we survived because we did not wear protective masks and inhaled all of the dusty material. After about three weeks the job was completed.

On the way back from the farm we decided to explore the surrounding area. Needing gas, pulled into a gas station in a small town of 2,000. Looked around and everyone in the community was black. They had established their own city in Missouri. They were delighted I stopped by for gas and a visit to their city. Couldn't believe my eyes, an all-black city just 15 miles from Pittsburg.

During my journey home, the brakes on my car quit working and I had to use the emergency brake to stop and start. Brakes going out on old cars were normal. It happened a lot.

Back home an unemployed started looking for another job and found one at the local drive-in theater. This was an enjoyable job and consisted of parking cars, selling tickets, and working in the concession stand. Worked there for about eight weeks before school started. Going to school all day and then working a nighttime job didn't seem a good idea. So, it was necessary to terminate the night job in favor of school.

1949 – Starting the Senior year at age 16 years old, was considering running for one of the senior class officer positions. Wait, everyone knows only popular students are class officers. Decided to do it anyway. Knew the President and Vice Presidents would be reserved for a superhero or cute girl. That left the offices of the

Secretary and Treasurer. Secretary didn't sound right for a boy, so running for Treasure was the choice. Maybe other students would be too intimidated to put their names in public view and face possible failure. Could I win by default? The ballot was published and had one competing for Treasurer. He was from the established in-crowd. All was lost, good try, at least my name was on the ballot. Election results were published and as expected the President was Captain of the Basketball Team and the Vice-President was a cute girl from the in-crowd. Wait, the Secretary elected was from the Blue Color group and I was elected Treasurer and outsider of both groups. This was like the Olympics. Didn't achieve GOLD but got on the podium.

I was amazed. I was also elected to other officer positions in numerous clubs. In fact, it seemed like I was winning elections for reasons unknown to me. I did lose one election. That was as Captain of the Band. I was in the band allegedly playing like the saxophone. But I could hardly read the music fast enough. The same old reading problem. Reading music was like reading a textbook. Really a slow process.

My exploits were expanded by driving away football and basketball games to cities about 30 miles away. My car was always overloaded with students going to the games. If a student wanted a ride, they had an open invitation. Going to one game we were stranded once when the car broke down on a two-lane unlit road. My side-kick mechanic let me down this one time. Most riders had to thumb their way to the game. This event just added to the adventure and mystics of the road warriors, no worries. These escapades and other activities drew a lot of attention, and it seemed like my name was in every issue of the school's weekly paper. A few reporters were among my riders seeking their own time in the limelight which was great fun to share. I mindlessly seemed to understand that you should never count yourself out of a venture. I progressed from the unknown to having the time of my life.

I Signed up for the Senior play and this time, got a humorous part. During the performance, I really got into my character, and extraneously started adlibbing original lines. The cast was stunned by the positive audience response. The Director insisted the additional lines be added to the next three performances. Of course, the school newspaper wrote a review of the play, and I was the only actor named and congratulated in the review. Being humble, I imagined talent scouts would be calling for me to co-star with John Wayne.

I got to meet John Wayne a few years later. Was working as a Captain in the Command-and-Control Center of the 1st Brigade of the 101st Airborne Division when contact was made with undesirables. After a few days of contact about 2,500 persons hostile to the government of South Vietnam were terminated. The event was written up in all the national media such as "Newsweek." John Wayne being an action guy came out to the jungle to visit the current generation of fighting men in their combat area. Few prominent dignitaries came to the field.

###

Being on the stage was exhilarating. There was a talent show coming up and the school wanted volunteers. Here was another opportunity for stage time and signed up. Now. I assumed the roles of writer, producer, director, and actor. Talked another student into participating in the skit. The skit was a simple production, and we decided on a Western theme. We brought our .22 caliber pistols, with blank ammunition, and had a shootout on stage. We ended the scene by singing a popular western song of the day called, "Mule Train."

###

There was one major school event left for the year, and that was the prom dance. Included in this final occurrence came the election of the Prom King and Queen. Those elected would get a full-page picture in the yearbook, front-page coverage in the local newspaper invited to business lunches, and a VIP tour of the college campus. A real town VIP for a few weeks. Again, I assumed that a person elected King would have to be a superstar in sports or music and have an "A" grade point average. Not sure who that person would be, and I, lacked superstar status and had a "C" plus grade point average. You only needed a" C" grade point average to graduate. You could have considered me an overachiever with a "C" plus. No worries, had adventures, freedom, car and a few people knew my name. My main concern about the prom was getting a date.

###

The weather was getting warmer, so the Math Department elected to have a morning breakfast for its students at a local park. Of course, was having a good time and missed the starting school bell. This was my first time missing High School in three years. High School was too much fun to miss even a day. However, since I was going to be late anyway, decided to take the morning off.

###

Feeling a little guilty, returned to school at lunchtime. Walking down the hall, I started receiving congratulations. Not knowing what this was about, finally stopped someone and asked. He had a puzzled look on his face, he didn't know I had skipped school that morning. He said, "You were elected King this morning and it was announced during the assembly." The girl elected Queen had been my mentor in my Sophomore year. Now, I would escort her to the prom ceremonies. The issue of getting a date was no longer a problem and there appeared to be an over choice of girls. Had previously dated a sophomore majorette a few times and she agreed to be my date. Ironically, she was elected Prom Queen in her senior year. We dated a few times in college, but I'm afraid my communication skills with girls were still lacking.

###

Had mentioned earlier that my name seemed to appear in almost every issue of the school newspaper. Curiosity finally got the best of me and went to the editor's room and read each issue. As it turned out, I appeared in 12 of the 16 issues. Eight of the articles included photos with three on the front page. One article forecasted that when I returned to the 15-year reunion, it would be as a world adventurer. It came to be! Spent two years in the Marine Corps in California, two years in Berlin, and traveled throughout Europe, one year in South Vietnam, and traveled throughout Asia. It's interesting how your future can be predicted at an early age.

###

Suddenly, it was graduation. It became necessary to find another date, with a senior girl, for graduation night parties. Most couples had already paired up and things looked bleak. Then one evening, after graduation rehearsal, I went outside and sat on the steps to enjoy the evening when a girl sat down beside me. She was the leader of the majorettes, and we had been on a few dates in the past two years. Again, my communication skills weren't that great. Surprised, she started talking and before the conversation hardly started asked me to take her out on graduation night. The date problem was solved. Had always been interested in her. Was this a clue the interest might be mutual, or did she just need a date? No matter the reason, my date for the senior evening was solved.

Didn't have a chance to follow up with the graduation night date. Two days later, left for western Kansas for the wheat harvest, to the town of Newton, 30 miles north of Wichita. A football player knew I liked adventure, so he invited me to go with him to Newton. He had relatives in the area who promised they would find us a job.

CHAPTER 5.

In 1950, after graduating high school at age 17, I headed to Newton, Kansas with my friend and classmate. We drove our separate cars in a convoy of two vehicles. His uncle, as promised, had jobs lined up when we got there. I ended up working for a religious Mennonite farmer. Going to harvest was a good job. Today, most of these jobs are filled by illegal immigrants or accomplished by huge harvesting corporations. The farmer leased his 200-300 acres. The initial job was the harvesting of the wheat. The farmer drove an old combine, and I drove a truck. When the wheat bin of the combine was full, I would pull the truck up alongside the combine and we would transfer the wheat to the truck. Then the full truck would be driven to a silo in town and offloaded. When the wheat harvest was completed, I assisted in the numerous jobs around the farm. For example, in the corn field, weeds were as high as the growing corn. The weeds had to be eliminated. One hot afternoon, in the Kansas summer heat, we cut each weed out by hand with a machete. The corn was as high as your head, so no breeze could be felt. There were other farming activities such as plowing and mowing grass in the fields. One afternoon, we were doing routine farming activities and I was driving a tractor with a trailer attached. While driving the tractor up a small incline in the farmer's yard the trailer became disconnected and was rolling towards the creek. The tractor was moving slowly, less than two MPH. My first reaction was to jump off the tractor and stop the trailer. So, I did. Then I realized I hadn't turned the motor off and now the unguided tractor was still running and slowly heading towards the farmer's wife's garden. I instinctively stopped and started to chase the tractor. The ignition key was located on the left side of the dash. To get to the key, you had to run in front of the large wheel of the tractor. Hastily, I jumped in front of the large moving wheel and thought I would walk in front of it while reaching for the ignition key to turn off the motor. I didn't reach the key in time, the rear wheel grabbed my foot pulling me to the ground, it ran over my leg up my back, and off my shoulder. Good thing it missed my head. I got up and tried it again. However, this time I stopped the tractor. Looking toward the trailer, I noticed the farmer had stopped it from smashing into the creek. He had an amused look on his face. Walking over to discuss what had happened, I told him that the tractor had run over me. Of course, he didn't believe that was possible. After a short conversation, I turned and walked away. Stunned, he now noticed the mud marks left by the tractor wheel up my back. He got excited, loaded me into the car, and rushed me to a local chiropractor. I had never heard of a chiropractor, but I was in no position to argue. After a few tugs and pulls, there was no physical damage, and I felt great. The dash to town was probably unnecessary, but the farmer was relieved.

###

My usual luck was holding out, because the night before, we had planned to put heavyweights on the wheels. These weights were installed when planning to pull a plow. The extra weight prevented the wheels from spinning under the added load while pulling a plow through the ground. Fortunately, livestock had broken out of the barn, and we had to round them up leaving no time to add weights. Otherwise, there would have been heavyweights on the wheels which would have resulted in my being squashed like a bug.

###

It seemed this tractor had it in for me. Later, I was pulling the tractor with a large trailer consisting of 50 or more sharp discs which served as wheels. The purpose of these disks was to cut the plowed lumps of dirt into smaller pieces thus leveling the ground after plowing. While pulling the discs I came across a low-hanging tree limb, and I thought I would again walk beside the tractor and steer to avoid being hit by the tree limbs. That would have put me in front of the big wheel again. If I had done that and had been run over by the tractor a second time, I wouldn't have been able to get up in time before the discs would have made bacon strips out of me.

That summer, while working on the farm, the Korean War started on June 25, 1950. North Korea had invaded South Korea. The United States had military forces in South Korea and were caught up in the fighting. We were involved. This seemed like a small conflict when compared to WW II, that had ended in 1945. The conflict didn't spark much interest. Just another news report.

###

After six weeks, the farm job ended, and I returned to Pittsburg. Thought I would look up my graduation night date. Before taking steps in that direction, I was told she had married a baseball player on the local professional team. In 1950, small towns had what could be called "C" teams. These were less talented athletes, but they made for great evening entertainment until replaced by TV. They had a boy and then divorced within a year. Twelve years later we ran into each other again in Pittsburg.

###

My dad was in the process of establishing a business in Springfield, Missouri about 80 miles east of Pittsburgh. With the rest of my summer free, my dad asked me to join him.

He was setting up an optical shop where customers could come to purchase eyeglasses with prescriptions from an optometrist. In addition to selling the glasses, he ground the glass to the desired specifications. He had all the required equipment in a second room.

The location of his office was on the second floor. There was no elevator in the building, so customers would have to climb the stairs.

His advertising comprised of large signs placed in the second-story windows. Overall, it was a poor location, but the rent was reasonable.

###

Only one person ventured to the second floor in response to his advertisement. I wasn't sure this venture was going to be a successful business. We also went to the county fair and set up a booth to sell sunglasses. We sold one pair. With no visible income from the business, my dad still seemed content and had plenty of money available.

###

The Korean War had been in progress for about a month and the people in the other booths started kidding me that I would be drafted soon for military service. To me, the war seemed small and irreverent. General MacArthur predicted a victory by Christmas. So, the draft seemed remote.

###

There was a small diner near my dad's office where we would go for breakfast. One morning I went to breakfast alone. At the diner, the people there said they had heard on the news that my dad had died. My dad and I were both living in the office, and I had just left him, so I chalked it up as an odd joke. However, the next week I went alone to breakfast and again, the regular patrons said they had heard, on the radio, that my dad died. This time they were correct. I thought it was interesting how I kept getting these reports every time I went to the restaurant. It led me to wonder where my dad was getting his money. After his death, my mom and I discovered a stack of money hidden in the office. With the money, there were many news clippings of me in the hometown newspaper. However, finding this money led to rumors of my dad being associated with the underworld. Nevertheless, the Coroner's Report said my dad died from a heart attack at age 42. According to reports, my dad was driving and had pulled off to check something on the car and had a sudden heart attack. The night before

Dad said he would like to go home at midweek. I discouraged him because we were going home anyway on the weekend. It would have been better if we had gone home at midweek.

###

With the summer finished, I started college in the fall of 1950 at age 17. College was inexpensive with tuition about 60 dollars for the semester and that included the loan of textbooks. Costs were further reduced because I was living at home, only a few blocks from campus. After enrolling, I was rushed by a fraternity. At that time, there were only two fraternities on campus and the one most Pittsburg students pledged was the Sigma Tau Gamma. I was surprised to get so much attention. The fraternity was just looking to increase its membership.

Having missed out on football in High School, I decided to try out for college football. The coach generously let anyone give it a try. Having no high school experience with the game was a predictable failure. I'm glad I tried out for the team.

###

Walking home one afternoon, I encountered an attractive black girl going my direction. We graduated high school together. We talked for a few blocks and then I turned off to go to my grandparents' house about two blocks away. Arriving at my grandparents' home, they greeted me with a slight reprimand. Word traveled fast. Walking with a black girl was almost considered as bad as dating a Catholic. For a small town of 20,000, Pittsburg had both a Protestant and a Catholic school. I believe my first encounter with a Catholic student was in college.

###

During my freshman year the BEST inherited eye problem really came on strong causing tremendous eye strain. As usual, I could see objects, but I felt like I was looking through poorly focused binoculars. This added to my already poor reading ability. I had no idea what was going on, but the eyestrain was overwhelming. This condition lasted for five years before it subsided significantly. Decades later, I learned that this is the pattern for BEST. Back home, my mom was struggling financially to raise three children with little money. She had taken the first available job and was earning 40 dollars a week. To help, I got a job delivering Western Union telegrams after school. My mode of transportation was a motor scooter that came with the job. It was an easy job in the fall, but in winter snow it became more of a challenge.

In 1950, the government notified families of military servicemen by telegram if a soldier was wounded, missing or killed. Those telegrams were delivered by the station manager. Twenty years later, during the Vietnam War, these telegrams were delivered by military officers. I delivered a few of these messages.

CHAPTER 6.

From the time I was assigned to Camp Pendleton in May 1951 until January 1952, we were organized to become the 3rd Marine Division. This Division was officially reactivated in January 1952. Prior to activation, I believe Brigadier General Chesty Puller (USMC icon) was the Commander, who retired a few years later as a Lieutenant General (3 Stars).

In the later part of 1951, I met Brigadier General Chesty Puller. I was a Private First Class (PFC) and a Machine Gun Squad Leader in his unit. One day he ordered an inspection of his entire command. This was an inspection of Marines standing in formation. The General passed in front of each Marine so he could observe each of them, and they could observe him. Upon his arrival, the entire unit came to attention. As the General passed in front, each Marine presented their rifle for inspection. He would stop to inspect some of the rifles or might just ask a question of the marine.

We were one of the last units to be inspected, and I could hear his voice at the other end of the parade field. I heard him responding to a complaint from a Marine's mother. She had complained that her son was living in tents and not barracks. He was responding to the complaint in a loud voice. He said if the mothers of America would ask Congress to appropriate more money, he would put the Marines in a Taj Mahal. When he arrived in front of me, I came to inspection arms with my rifle. I looked and was surprised to see how short he was for having such a loud voice. I'm not sure how tall he was, but I thought I was looking at the top of his head. Interestingly, 28 years later I worked for Brigadier General Puller's Aide at United States Forces Japan Headquarters, a Joint Headquarters near Tokyo whose staff has Army, Navy, Marine, and Air Force personnel. His Aide had been promoted from Lieutenant to Major General (2 Stars) and was now serving as Deputy commander of the command.

###

It was Christmas of 1951. We had the option of a 10-day leave during Christmas or New Year's. I and one of the guys I enlisted with from Pittsburg, Kansas elected the Christmas option. We used the Frazer car. We announced we were headed in that direction and had six empty seats. Immediately, we had six more passengers. Pittsburg was 1,600 miles, with about 1,400 miles down the famous Route 66. We drove our overloaded car straight for 36 hours to cover the distance. We only stopped for gas and got our food at the gas station. On our return trip, it was the same story. I'm surprised we made it without incident.

We returned prior to the New Year and took advantage of the extra time off. Several of us hopped into my car and went to the Rose Bowl Parade. The Grand Marshal for 1952 was Hopalong Cassidy, a popular movie and TV cowboy. At the parade, I met a couple of other Marines from my high school. We all joined together and went to the Rose Bowl football game. College participants were Stafford (7) vs Illinois (40)

###

In April 1952, they were doing an atomic bomb test in the Nevada desert, and they included Marines. The purpose was to demonstrate to the United States military it was possible to survive and fight in a nuclear environment. The Marines dug in three miles from ground zero. Our company was designated to provide one-half of its Marines for the test. They asked for volunteers and almost everyone did.

Again, I volunteered but wasn't selected. Since almost 100 percent volunteered, I believe they arbitrarily chose those to participate. Seemed like I was always missing out. I was not selected for Korea or the atomic test. Maybe I was lucky after all. Had I participated, I could have gotten a good dose of radiation. Everything was experimental at that time and sometimes the outcomes were unknown.

###

In the Battalion area, the Marine Corps built a small wooden temporary building where beer and pre-packaged sandwiches were sold. It was small but had a few tables and chairs for customers. One night too much beer was consumed and those drinking became unruly, and started tearing up the furniture, throwing beer cans, and scuffling. The Officer of the Day was called. As soon as he arrived, he was hit over the head with a beer bottle and knocked unconscious. The next morning the battalion was standing at attention while the Officer of the Day passed by each Marine to see if he could identify anyone from the previous night's encounter. No luck, that's almost an impossible task since we were all about the same age, with the same haircut and in the same uniform. To my surprise, the beer hall reopened that evening, minus furniture. The furniture was never replaced. If you wanted to stay inside, you could sit on the floor. In many places, the establishment would have been closed for weeks or permanently. Not in the Marine Corps. That impressed me as a 19-year-old.

###

One thing I wanted to do in the military was to go through the Infiltration Course. That's where you crawl under barbed wire while a machine gun fires real ammunition three feet over your head. The day finally arrived, and we were the second company in line to go through. Unfortunately, while the first company was going through, the machine gun became loose in its mount and started spraying bullets among the Marines crawling under the wire. Fortunately, only one Marine was hit in the rear end and survived, but that suspended all training for the day, and I never had another opportunity. It seems I always missed out!

One dark morning, I was marching to breakfast in company formation, a sleepy 18-year-old, driving a two-and-one-half ton truck, didn't notice he was entering a 10 MPH troop area. Ahead of him was the company formation. At the last second, he saw the company and swerved off the road hitting the last eight Marines in the formation. No one was killed and the eight were injured and qualified for rest and relaxation in the hospital.

###

When I enlisted in the Marine Corps, my goal was to serve only during war. This put me in the category of an active-duty reservist. Early in the Korean War many Reservists from WW II were called to active duty. Because of my reserve category I was lumped in with the WW II Reservists.

###

By early 1952 the draft was fully operational, and Reservists were no longer needed and were ordered to return to their homes. Here I am just 16 months in the Marine Corps, with a war still on, being told I was no longer needed and would be discharged back to my hometown in May 1952.

Before leaving active duty as a reservist, I was interviewed by a Major who was recruiting young reservists to change their reserve status to Regular. He asked me what I planned to do. I said, that since the G.I. Bill had just recently been reinstated for Korean Veterans, I would return to college. However, I told him I would sign on as a Regular if he would ensure I would receive immediate orders to Korea. He smiled, got up from behind his desk, and escorted me out of the tent in a polite fashion. He told me to go back to school. This was an unusual act by a Marine Corps officer. I was disappointed. It seemed like it was impossible to get to a war zone. The war was passing me by. Though disappointed, there was still the jubilation that I was free to move on to other adventures.

###

Interestingly, before my enlistment into the Marine Corps, the US Army reserve artillery battery in Pittsburgh, Kansas tried to recruit me. They promised I would be able to complete college without going to Korea. I should have joined because they were activated and did go to Korea. I joined the Marine Corps thinking that was a sure thing to Korea, but I ended up at Camp Pendleton, California.

###

There were several other Reservists in my Platoon being discharged at the same time headed East. I offered them a ride in my Frazer to Joplin, Missouri. This is a town 30 miles from Pittsburg and had good connecting trains and buses to their destinations. I can say it was a joyous trip and we were all delighted to be free. We made several stops along the way visiting tourist attractions such as the Petrified Forest, the government boneyard for WW II aircraft and Indian Mountain Dwellings.

###

Returning home, the last week in May of 1952, I decided to look for a job. A friend of my mom lived in Dodge City, Kansas, and said her husband could get me a job during wheat harvest. I accepted the invitation and caught a bus to Dodge City. Her husband had great connections and I ended up working for the largest farmer in the area. The farmer and his sons owned or leased most of the county farmland. During the Depression and "Dust Bowl" days of the 1930's the farmer and his family survived by raising turkeys along the Cimarron River. I ended up working for his son who had been a Navy fighter pilot during WW II.

After four weeks the job was finished, and I caught a return bus to Pittsburg. As I boarded the bus, I was amazed to see my unescorted Granddad. The one who had lost his eyesight in a mining accident a few years earlier. We had a great visit for 300 miles.

###

Returning home, I started looking for a job. My mom had gotten a job at a Kansas Army Ammunition plant in Parson, Kansas a couple of years earlier. They were producing ammunition for the Korean War. I decided to apply for a security officer position at the plant. I thought they would be delighted to have a 19-year-old ex-Marine. However, they considered me a little immature for the job. Another job offer was to walk behind a chemical fertilizer truck to level out the fertilizer as the truck dumped it on the ground. After that was an offer from a coal equipment manufacturing company to shovel coal into the furnace, keeping it hot for molding metal. Finally, I got a job pumping gasoline at a service station. The service station was located about six blocks from home and two blocks from the college. I could go to college during the day and work the evening shift.

In the 1950s, gas was pumped by a service attendant who also washed your windows. Additionally, you could ask them to check your oil level and tire pressure. No self-service was available.

When college started in the fall of 1952, it was time to select a course of study. At the time, it seemed the only acceptable courses were doctor, lawyer, or engineer. I didn't care much for any of them, but I had done well in math, so I enrolled in pre-engineering. You could take two years at Kansas State Teachers College but would have to transfer to an engineering school to finish the four-year degree. At that time the cost was $60 a semester and they loaned you the books. Basically, college was free except you had to pay room and board. Students living in town stayed with their parents. With school starting I rejoined the fraternity, the Sigma Tau Gamma. As I was enrolled in engineering, I decided to join the Engineer Club. During the Engineer Club's first meeting, I was elected President. With this position came the requirement to organize several field trips to mining and manufacturing companies. We organized three field trips during the semester, the first one was to an underground lead and zinc mine In

Missouri. It ran for miles underground and had at least a 50-foot ceiling. They had large dump trucks driving underground. These trucks were designed so the exhaust emissions were neutralized. It was an unbelievable operation and near my hometown. Another trip was to the Sheffield Steel manufacturing factory near Kansas City. They walked us through the whole process of the steel-making business. The final trip was to the Cessna airplane manufacturing plant in Wichita, Kansas. College was turning out to be another great adventure. I could visualize working 40 hours a week at the gas station, attending class 15 hours a week and studies associated with college wasn't a good formula for success. Accordingly, I dropped the gas station job. I still had my G.I. Bill education income of 110 dollars a month. That was a good sum in 1952.

CHAPTER 7.

Because we had been traveling on a train for two nights, we were a sad-looking group when we got off the bus from the train station. Disembarking from the bus we were greeted by our future Drill Instructor (D.I.). These greetings are not happy events and our egos were deflated, leaving us feeling two feet tall. After about 30 minutes of standing at attention, we gathered up our suitcases and attempted to march to the receiving barracks. The rest of the day was filled with endless tasks. No jobs were ever considered completed satisfactorily.

The next morning, we gathered up all our belongings and were marched to the supply room area to turn in our personal effects and receive uniforms and field equipment. We entered a large empty room. Our first assignment was to put all our belongings into a large bag for storage. That included all the clothing we were wearing. We were in our birthday suits. Being stripped prevented anyone from concealing any civilian items or weapons, such as, knifes, brass knuckles, black jacks, or pistols. The recruits were from all backgrounds. Everyone was to start equally.

After packing, and standing in our birthday suits, we started moving through a line to get our uniforms. The first item we got was boots without socks. As we were stumbling along, we got instructions to check the size of the boots to our feet. Whoever was in charge realized that was not a smart idea and reversed his decision by instructing everyone to take off the boots but keep the line moving. In my typical Kansas style, I was moving too slow while following the boots-on and boots-off instructions. While I was bent over and slowly removing my boots, I got a big boot kick right to my bare rear end. That got my attention as I sprawled out on the floor. After getting fully outfitted we proceeded for the haircut. This was a shaving of the head.

Having gotten our haircut, uniform, and equipment we were ready for training. We were now ready to be real recruits and were taken to the recruit barracks and assigned to our bunks. The bunks were stacked two beds high, consisting of a metal frame strung with wire springs to hold the person sleeping. On top, you were issued a rolled-up mattress that you carried and placed on the bunk. It worked well and was comfortable, no need for a thousand-dollar bed. The recruit who bunked above me had been a Navy pilot in WW II. His brother had been killed early in the Korean War. He wanted revenge and enlisted as a Marine recruit so he could go to Korea as a rifleman. People did that in 1951.

The next event was academic testing. My score was high, well over that required for Officer Candidate School (OCS). At 18 years old, this was confusing, because in Pittsburg I had misunderstood my 100 score to be an I.Q. test.

After the testing, two other recruits and I, in our platoon of about 90, scored high enough to take an advanced test. I missed passing this test by one point. There were several physics questions. If I had answered one more correctly, I would have passed. I should have taken physics in high school. No one explained the purpose of the test. As far as being an officer, I was too young to qualify. Officers had to be at least 19 years old.

The next step was talking to an assignment NCO. He asked what job I wanted in the Marine Corps. When I enlisted in Joplin, I told the recruiter I wanted to be a tail gunner on a dive bomber. The recruiter said ten percent went into aviation. Of course, I didn't stop to think that included the mechanics, pilots, and everyone participating in aviation. So, when the assignment NCO asked, this was my choice I told him my desire was to be a tail gunner on a dive bomber. He told me that Marine dive bombers went out withn World War II. No more gunner positions. So, I said I wanted to be a Marine Raider. He said the Raiders went out with World War II also. So, I said I want to be a paratrooper. He said the Marines don't have paratroopers. Finally, I gave up and said I wanted to be a rifleman. He was delighted and that made his job easy because every Marine is a rifleman. To clarify, a rifleman is in the Infantry. Therefore, off to the infantry I went.

During training, we had one wise guy. The drill instructors finally got tired of his attitude. He called the Marine recruit front and center. He gave the platoon an order of about-face (facing to the rear). Then I heard a thump, somebody fell to the ground. We did another about-face (facing to the front) we saw the wise guy laid out sprawled on the drill field. The drill instructor gave some excuses, and they called an ambulance. We never saw him again. On another occasion, we were doing rifle drills in the barracks because of bad weather. One recruit was a little slow. The Drill Instructor (D.I.) then reprimanded him in a loud manner. Disgusted at the recruit, the D.I. threw his hard hat at him. The recruit trembled then collapsed and fell to the floor. I think they took him to the psycho ward -- didn't see him anymore. We had two or three more that were evacuated, never to be seen again.

In 1951, quitting wasn't an option. Once you signed up for the military you were government property. I believe today it's different.

Part of the 10-week training program was conducted at Camp Matthews Rifle Range near San Diego. You spent three weeks there for rifle marksmanship training. There we stayed in tents and spent most of our time on the range. On the rifle range, I scored the highest score in my tent.

On the range, the mess hall must've gotten careless in handling the food because everyone got dysentery. It was also the flu season, and I got a cold or the flu. But I wasn't about to go on sick call because they would probably keep you a couple of days to recover. This meant that you would be set back a week and put into a different platoon one week behind.

In the adjacent tent, one of the recruits apparently wasn't keeping proper hygiene. Some of his buddies decided to give him a blanket party. Covered by a blanket, the person under the blanket is hit several times. When he quits resisting, they dragged him from the tent to the shower where they used scrub brushes on him.

###

Finally, it was graduation day. On this day there is a drill competition between other platoons graduating on the same day. This drill was included as part of the overall graduation ceremony. Of course, we were told we were ranked first in the competition. But I noticed on our group picture this rating wasn't annotated. Since it's the last day, and you're on your way to 10 days leave, no one has the desire or time to recheck. I thought every drill instructor told his platoon they were first.

###

In April 1951, I returned home with a 10-day leave. While visiting, I was invited to a party of a wealthy family in Pittsburg. I knew her son and believe the family wanted to be patriotic and support our military effort. Being a naïve Swede I didn't realize what an important event this was and declined.

###

In May 1951, two buddies and I were assigned to Camp Pendleton, California. One of us was assigned to the artillery and the other two of us were assigned to the infantry. We did our training in a camp just east of San Clemente, California. The hills overlooking the shore were all grass in 1951. When returning for a visit, in 1990 the hills were dotted with condos. San Clemente later became President Nixon's second White House during his presidency.

Our unit of assignment was the newly forming 3rd Marine division to be commanded by Brigadier General Chesty Puller (a Marine icon). This was a stateside unit and didn't deploy to Korea while I was assigned to the organization. A year later it was deployed to Japan.

Upon signing in from leave and now present for duty, I was assigned to the machine gun platoon of an infantry company. Strangely, we were all Private First Class (PFC), therefore, the company needed some PFC's to fill Sergeant leadership positions. This worked out, but nothing can replace an NCO for leadership and experience.

###

With the Korean War came the rapid expansion of the Marine Corps. This sudden growth resulted in a shortage of barracks. To solve this problem, the newly forming division was placed in six-man tents. From our viewpoint, this was great because they were easy to keep clean. Just sweep the dust out and roll up the tent flaps. That was it. The tent was heated by a small kerosene stove in cool weather. However, we had no electricity and used a kerosene lantern for lighting. After a few months, we received electricity and had one light bulb.

A couple of months later they did ask for volunteers for Korea. Everyone volunteered except 5 married Marines. Only 10 volunteers were selected. I wasn't one.

###

I remember at one formation; the First Sergeant was giving us some advice before going on weekend liberty. There had been several occasions when young Marines would be in San Diego or Los Angeles and get loaded on alcohol. In the darkly lit nightclub, he would find a girl, fall in love and get married on the weekend. The First Sergeant's recommendation, before you get married, was to take the girl to the beach, put her in a swimsuit, and take her swimming. Observe her in the sunlight in a wetsuit, with wet hair and no makeup, this is an opportunity to verify her age. Chances are you will reconsider the marriage option.

He also lectured about a military career and the numerous benefits, medical benefits for life, a great retirement, and the ability for rapid promotion. Four years later that lecture resonated. To me, it seemed like a good idea. I could retire in 20 years, take my pension at age 40, and live in Central or South America like a king. However, getting married would alter this plan. If married and I was injured, I would get a pension for life. If I was killed, my wife would get a pension for life. Considering my dad died at 42 leaving my mom with three children and no money, the military pension and medical benefits were a super deal.

CHAPTER 8.

During my time in the Marine Corps, I got to participate in one amphibious landing. It was right out of the World War II movies. While aboard ship, I remember they said you must clean your rifle every day in the saltwater atmosphere, or it will rest. Of course, I didn't and waited a couple days. I had a rusty mess.

###

When it was time to make the beach assault, we went over the side of the ship by rope netting to board a smaller landing craft, it seemed simple to climb down a rope net, except when you get to the bottom you noticed that the landing craft was bobbing up and down in 5-to-10-foot swells. You had to wait till it was at the top of the swell to jump from the net to the landing craft. Otherwise, you could fall 5 or 10 feet.

###

The Navy used an island off the coast of California as their practice assault beach. After the rehearsal, we returned to the ship, in ours. To get on board you had to climb back up the same rope netting you used to get off the ship. Climbing up the net looked easy, however, with your rifle and gear weighing about 60 pounds, this proved to be a bigger challenge than expected. First, you had to time the 10-foot water swells and at the top of the swell to grab the rope netting. If you grabbed the net at the bottom of the swell, you could get crushed between the landing craft and ship as they came together at the top of the next swell. Secondly, the landing craft had to maneuver close enough for you to grab the rope netting dangling to the side of the ship. Thirdly, you must climb the net for 20 to 30 feet to get on board with several troops on the net at the same time. It was a slow process waiting on the person above you. By the time you got to the top, you could barely hang on because of the exhaustion caused by the extended time on the net, and the bobbing and weaving of the ship while holding on to the rope net.

###

A couple of days later we made the actual assault on Camp Pendleton beach, where we used the Marine amphibious tracked vehicle. We went down to the well of the ship where the vehicles were located and loaded aboard. When it was time for the assault, the ship lowered a ramp in the bow of the ship and the vehicles were driven off the ramp into the ocean. All the hatches on the vehicle are closed because sometimes the vehicle sinks below the surface for a short time before bobbing up. They are not supposed to sink, but on a rare occasion, one does. This was an apprehensive moment.

Out we went and we floated okay. The vehicle proceeded to the beach where we drove onto it with our tracked vehicles. As we disembarked, we encountered a Marine Corps' historical tradition. Publicity! There was a barrier of invited TV and movie cameras, and newspaper and magazine reporters. We maneuvered our way through the flashing bulbs of the cameras and continued our three-day field exercise associated with the amphibious landing.

###

We were at training one day and another Marine and I decided to skip out and go back to our tents and goof off. We didn't think we would be missed. When the platoon returned the platoon leader (who had been a Marine Raider, a special unit in World War II) called me to his tent. I thought I was in deep trouble. When I got there, he said he had fired one of the squad leaders and that I was his replacement. I don't know if they knew I had skipped training or not. But being designated as squad leader was certainly a good punishment. That way he could keep track of me easily and I would be responsible for keeping track of the squad members. And to top it off, we all held the rank of Private First Class (PFC) and I was the youngest in my group by one or two years. In the Platoon, we had six Machine Gun Squads. Now, I was one of the squad leaders.

###

As a squad leader, I received additional duties such as "charge of quarters" at night. In this position, you were given a guard detail of six Marines, who were to keep order in the company area and serve as fire watch. Each tent had a small oil stove and sometimes the heat adjustment would fail, and the stove would get red hot setting a tent on fire.

One night I had the duty and oversaw six assigned guards. All went well. The next morning everyone was going to breakfast except my guards who were still on fire watch. I decided to go send them to breakfast even though they had another hour of duty. Of course, as soon as they left, a tent caught on fire. Fortunately, no one was in it. They had all gone to breakfast. Again, I thought I was in deep trouble having dismissed my guards before their end of tour that day. I called the fire department and directed them to the fire, and everything went well. I was sure I was going to be called on the carpet, but nothing happened.

In the summer of 1951, I would hitchhike to Los Angeles on the weekends. A friend of mine from high school was there, working in construction. He had bought a 1940s, very stylish Packard convertible. He and I would tour the Los Angeles clubs. We got to see Tennessee Ernie Ford, Harry James, Lawrence Welk, Les Brown, and "His band of Renown" and many others.

Before coming to California and still in high school, the two of us were looking for something to do and attended a church weekend retreat in a nearby town. At one of the beaches near Los Angeles, we met one of the girls who had been at the retreat. She took us home to meet her parents. They were shocked to see a Marine bringing their daughter home. I explained that I had just turned 18 but looked older in uniform. I think the girl was 16. The parents were good-natured about the event and responded by taking everyone for a drive-in sandwich and a tour of the area.

Hitchhiking was against the Marine Corps rules, but I did. The $80 monthly pay didn't leave much money for transportation. One time I was hitchhiking to Los Angeles and a person stopped and picked me up in San Clemente. The girl driver looked quite strange. Supposedly it was a woman, but if it was a woman, it was the ugliest that I had ever seen. I was still naïve and didn't believe all this gender confusion stuff that I had heard. This looked like a guy in a dress with makeup on. Fortunately for me, the military police saw me hitchhiking and stopped the car, and got me out. Again, I thought I was in deep trouble hitchhiking. The military police were going to the train station in Los Angeles and gave me a ride. One afternoon I was on the San Clemente beach, a couple of miles from our camp and I met a girl and her parents from San Bernardino. She agreed to give her address/ San Bernardino is 70 miles from camp. One Sunday, on the spur of the moment, I decided to hitchhike to San Bernardino to visit the girl, without calling ahead. That didn't go too well. I did notice that the girl had her hair in rollers and the conversation made for an uncomfortable visit. Therefore, I decided to start hitchhiking back. This mode of transportation can take a long time while waiting for someone to pick you up. It was getting dark and cold, I thought I would never get a ride back to Camp Pendleton. Finally, after getting three or four short rides I made it back at 2:00 A.M.

###

Sometimes I would have free time, and I would hang out at the local marina lying on one of the benches and looking up at the small civilian airplanes flying overhead. I would have given anything for a flight in one of these aircraft. I still wanted to be in aviation as a member of a flight crew.

###

In the military, you get 30 days a year of leave or vacation. We were taking these leaves in 10-day stretches. On the first trip home, I traveled by train. On the second trip in September 1951, I hitched a ride on a Marine Corps transport airplane at Miramar Marine Air Station in San Diego to Dallas, Texas. From Dallas, I had to take the bus. On the return trip, I picked up the family's Frazer and traveled down the famous Route 66 which connected Chicago to Los Angeles. The Frazer car was one of two cars we had in the family. Having hitch-hiked myself, I was willing to pick up hitchhikers. The first hitchhiker I picked up was a man about 45 years old. He was going to California to co-locate with the rest of his family. he was a nice guy and I'm glad I picked him up. Outside of Denver, in front of the VA hospital, were two younger hitchhikers wearing pieces of military clothing. Since they were outside of the VA, it appeared they could've been veterans. Upon picking them up, I became convinced they weren't veterans and were using the VA as a backdrop to get a ride. It became obvious they were after my car and wanted to get rid of me any way they could. The only thing that slowed them down was my other passenger. They could have overpowered me if I was solo. They weren't big enough to take on me and my other older passenger. When we stopped along the road for a rest break, one asked me about an object on a nearby hill that I couldn't see. They said it went behind the hill and looked suspicious. They said the three of us should check it out, leaving the older passenger with the car. That was a red flag, and I declined. If I had gone, I wouldn't have come back. I finally got rid of them, leaving them at a gas station that had a restaurant. They were hungry and focused on food and demanding I buy. I told them I would buy. While waiting for the order to arrive the older passenger and I slipped out of the restaurant and drove away. Later he mailed me a check to offset my expenses.

###

One of my squad member's cousins was Mitzi Gaynor, the movie actress, singer, and dancer. In one of her roles, she co-starred with Bing

Crosby in the movie "White Christmas." My squad members' hobby was keeping track of Hollywood celebrities. He noticed that Marilyn Monroe was due to come to Camp Pendleton with a USO show. I had my Frazer automobile that would seat 8 people. We loaded 11 in the seats and the trunk and went to the show which was to be at 8 PM. We arrived at noon and acquired front-row seats. Marilyn Monroe came out as the last performer. She certainly lived up to everyone's expectations. She was tightly zipped up in a shiny, golden gown. She sang a couple of songs that ended the show. My friend, and I with other squad members decided to go up on the stage, uninvited. The military police were surprised, and it took them a while to get organized. During the chaos, one of my squad members edged closer to Marilyn and tried to get to the zipper on the gown. In the meantime, we were sharing the stage with Marilyn Monroe.

.

CHAPTER 9.

From the time I was assigned to Camp Pendleton in May 1951 until January 1952, we were organized to become the 3rd Marine Division. This Division was officially reactivated in January 1952. Prior to activation, I believe Brigadier General Chesty Puller (USMC icon) was the Commander, who retired a few years later as a Lieutenant General (3 Stars).

In the later part of 1951, I met Brigadier General Chesty Puller. I was a Private First Class (PFC) and a Machine Gun Squad Leader in his unit. One day he ordered an inspection of his entire command. This was an inspection of Marines standing in formation. The General passed in front of each Marine so he could observe each of them, and they could observe him. Upon his arrival, the entire unit came to attention. As the General passed in front, each Marine presented their rifle for inspection. He would stop to inspect some of the rifles or might just ask a question of the marine.

We were one of the last units to be inspected, and I could hear his voice at the other end of the parade field. I heard him responding to a complaint of a Marine's mother. She had complained that her son was living in tents and not barracks. He was responding to the complaint in a loud voice. He said if the mothers of America would ask Congress to appropriate more money, he would put the Marines in a Taj Mahal. When he arrived in front of me, I came to inspection arms with my rifle. I looked and was surprised to see how short he was for having such a loud voice. I'm not sure how tall he was, but I thought I was looking at the top of his head. Interestingly, 28 years later I worked for Brigadier General Puller's Aide at United States Forces Japan Headquarters, a Joint Headquarters near Tokyo whose staff has Army, Navy, Marine, and Air Force personnel. His Aide had been promoted from Lieutenant to Major General (2 Stars) and was now serving as Deputy commander of the command.

###

It was Christmas of 1951. We had the option of a 10-day leave during Christmas or New Year's. I and one of the guys I enlisted with from Pittsburg, Kansas elected the Christmas option. We used the Frazer car. We announced we were headed in that direction and had six empty seats. Immediately, we had six more passengers. Pittsburg was 1,600 miles, with about 1,400 miles down the famous Route 66. We drove our overloaded car straight for 36 hours to cover the distance. We only stopped for gas and got our food at the gas station. On our return trip, it was the same story. I'm surprised we made it without incident.

We returned before the New Year and took advantage of the extra time off. Several of us hopped into my car and went to the Rose Bowl Parade. The Grand Marshal for 1952 was Hopalong Cassidy, a popular movie and TV cowboy. At the parade, I met a couple of other Marine's from my high school. We all joined together and went to the Rose Bowl football game. College participants were Stafford (7) vs Illinois (40)

###

In April 1952, they were doing an atomic bomb test in the Nevada desert, and they included Marines. The purpose was to demonstrate to the United States military it was possible to survive and fight in a nuclear environment. The Marines dug in three miles from ground zero. Our company was designated to provide one-half of its Marines for the test. They asked for volunteers and almost everyone did.

Again, I volunteered but wasn't selected. Since almost 100 percent volunteered, I believe they arbitrarily chose those to participate. Seemed like I was always missing out. I was not selected for Korea or the atomic test. Maybe I was lucky after all. Had I participated, I could have gotten a good dose of radiation. Everything was experimental at that time and sometimes the outcomes were unknown.

###

In the Battalion area, the Marine Corps built a small wooden temporary building where beer and pre-package sandwiches were sold. It was small but had a few tables and chairs for customers. One night too much beer was consumed and those drinking became unruly, and started tearing up the furniture, throwing beer cans, and scuffling. The Officer of the Day was called. As soon as he arrived, he was hit on the head with a beer bottle and knocked unconscious. The next morning the battalion was standing at attention while the Officer of the Day passed by each Marine to see if he could identify anyone from the previous night's encounter. No luck, that's almost an impossible task since we were all about the same age, with the same haircut and in the same uniform. To my surprise, the beer hall reopened that evening, without furniture. The furniture was never replaced. If you wanted to stay inside, you could sit on the floor. In many places, the establishment would have been closed for weeks or permanently. Not in the Marine Corps. That impressed me as a 19-year-old.

###

One thing I wanted to do in the military was to go through the Infiltration Course. That's where you crawl under barbed wire while a machine gun fires real ammunition three feet over your head. The day finally arrived, and we were the second company in line to go through. Unfortunately, while the first company was going through, the machine gun became loose in its mount and started spraying bullets among the Marines crawling under the wire. Fortunately, only one Marine was hit in the rear end and survived, but that suspended all training for the day, and I never had another opportunity. It seems I always missed out!

One dark morning, I was marching to breakfast in company formation, a sleepy 18-year-old, driving a two-and-one-half ton truck, didn't notice he was entering a 10 MPH troop area. Ahead of him was the company formation. At the last second, he saw the company and swerved off the road hitting the last eight Marines in the formation. No one was killed and the eight injured and qualified for rest and relaxation in the hospital.

###

When I enlisted in the Marine Corps, my goal was to serve only during war. This put me in the category of an active-duty reservist. Early in the Korean War many Reservists from WW II were called to active duty. Because of my reserve category, I was lumped in with the WW II Reservists.

###

By early 1952 the draft was fully operational, and Reservists were no longer needed and were ordered to return to their homes. Here I am just 16 months in the Marine Corps, with a war still on, being told I was no longer needed and would be discharged back to my hometown in May 1952.

Before leaving active duty as a reservist, I was interviewed by a Major who was recruiting young reservists to change their reserve status to Regular. He asked me what I planned to do. I said that since the G.I. Bill had just recently been reinstated for Korean Veterans, I would return to college. However, I told him I would sign on as a Regular if he would ensure I would receive immediate orders to Korea. He smiled, got up from behind his desk, and escorted me out of the tent in a polite fashion. He told me to go back to school. This was an unusual act by a Marine Corps officer. I was disappointed. It seemed like it was impossible to get to a war zone. The war was passing me by. Though disappointed, there was still the jubilation that I was free to move on to other adventures.

###

Interestingly, before my enlistment into the Marine Corps, the US Army reserve artillery battery in Pittsburgh, Kansas tried to recruit me. They promised I would be able to complete college without going to Korea. I should have joined because they were activated and did go to Korea. I joined the Marine Corps thinking that was a sure thing for Korea, but I ended up at Camp Pendleton, California.

###

There were several other Reservists in my Platoon being discharged at the same time headed East. I offered them a ride in my Frazer to Joplin, Missouri. This is a town 30 miles from Pittsburg and had good connecting trains and buses to their destinations. I can say it was a joyous trip and we were all delighted to be free. We made several stops along the way visiting tourist attractions such as the Petrified Forest, the government boneyard for WW II aircraft, and Indian Mountain Dwellings.

###

Returning home, the last week in May of 1952, I decided to look for a job. A friend of my mom lived in Dodge City, Kansas, and said her husband could get me a job during wheat harvest. I accepted the invitation and caught a bus to Dodge City. Her husband had great connections, and I ended up working for the largest farmer in the area. The farmer and his sons owned or leased most of the county farmland. During the Depression and "Dust Bowl" days of the 1930's the farmer and his family survived by raising turkeys along the Cimarron River. I ended up working for his son who had been a Navy fighter pilot during WW II.

After four weeks the job was finished, and I caught a return bus to Pittsburg. As I boarded the bus, I was amazed to see my unescorted Granddad. The one who had lost his eyesight in a mining accident a few years earlier. We had a great visit for 300 miles.

###

Returning home, I started looking for a job. My mom had gotten a job at a Kansas Army Ammunition plant in Parson, Kansas a couple of years earlier. They were producing ammunition for the Korean War. I decided to apply for a security officer position at the plant. I thought they would be delighted to have a 19-year-old ex-Marine. However, they considered me a little immature for the job. Another job offer was to walk behind a chemical fertilizer truck to level out the fertilizer as the truck dumped it on the ground. After that was an offer from a coal equipment manufacturing company to shovel coal into the furnace, keeping it hot for molding metal. Finally, I got a job pumping gasoline at a service station. The service station was located about six blocks from home and two blocks from the college. I could go to college during the day and work the evening shift.

In the 1950's, gas was pumped by a service attendant who also washed your windows. Additionally, you could ask them to check your oil level and tire pressure. No self-service was available.

###

When college started in the fall of 1952, it was time to select a course of study. At the time, it seemed the only acceptable courses were doctor, lawyer, or engineer. I didn't care much for any of them, but I had done well in math, so I enrolled in pre-engineering. You could take two years at Kansas State Teachers College but would have to transfer to an engineering school to finish the four-year degree. At that time the cost was $60 a semester and they loaned you the books. College was free except you had to pay for room and board. Students living in town stayed with their parents.

With school starting I rejoined the fraternity, the Sigma Tau Gamma. As I was enrolled in engineering, I decided to join the Engineer Club. During the Engineer Club's first meeting, I was elected President.

With this position came the requirement to organize several field trips to mining and manufacturing companies. We organized three field trips during the semester, the first one was to an underground lead and zinc mine In Missouri. It ran for miles underground and had at least a 50-foot ceiling. They had large dump trucks driving underground. These trucks were designed so the exhaust emissions were neutralized. It was an unbelievable operation and near my hometown. Another trip was to the Sheffield Steel manufacturing factory near Kansas City. They walked us through the whole process of the steel-making business. The final trip was to the Cessna airplane manufacturing plant in Wichita, Kansas.

###

College was turning out to be another great adventure. I could visualize working 40 hours a week at the gas station, attending class 15 hours a week and studies associated with college wasn't a good formula for success. Accordingly, I dropped the gas station job. I still had my G.I. Bill education income of 110 dollars a month. That was a good sum in 1952.

.

CHAPTER 10.

Leaving the Marine Corps in May 1952, I became an inactive reservist who still can be called up for active duty. After enrolling in college, I decided to join an active Marine Corps Reserve unit in Joplin, Missouri. In this unit, I was finally promoted to Corporal. While there, I was dismayed to see Marines collecting toys to give to children at Christmas in uniform. Arguably, this is good publicity within the local community, but I envisioned that a Marine should be portrayed as a flawless and fierce fighter. What enemy would be afraid of a Marine playing with toys. Doing this out of uniform would be okay and, no doubt, a worthy cause as well as an early recruitment of seven-year-olds.

###

The First Sergeant suggested everyone keep a personal file of all orders, promotions, medical, and financial records. His theory is that your records would be hard to locate in a few years. This Sergeant's advice was excellent for both military and civilian occupations. I would further advise that records should be saved as paper copies even in the digital age. I would also recommend that everyone keep a personal diary. Each week briefly summarize your activities for that week. In 20 or 30 years this information will become valuable.

###

At school, I was still having trouble with my inherited vision and hearing problems. It made it very difficult to read the blackboard and understand the accent of some instructors. As mentioned earlier, I can see objects but not detail. I can see the page of a book, but to focus on a specific word is difficult and stressful. This problem also creates poor face recognition. Listing to different dialects is difficult and if there is more than one noise, they cancel each other out and become one intelligible. For example, it is seldom that I can identify the lyrics of a song. I didn't realize I had a hearing problem until I was 49 years old. My wife was a teacher and counselor and tested elementary students' hearing acuity. She asked me to be the subject of the test so she could rehearse the testing procedure. I had the lowest score in, the 'Word Auditory Discrimination and Perception' (WADT) test.

These were minor problems and not a big deal. Everyone faces obstacles, so I thought these were unique problems encountered. For example, this vision problem is prevalent in one percent of the Swedish population, of course, I am Swedish. I wasn't diagnosed with the BEST hereditary eye disease until I was 53 years old. Medicine has made progress in diagnosing this problem in the past 30 years. Today, it is identifiable at an early age and disqualifies you for military service.

###

Searching for a solution I eventually was referred to the VA in Little Rock, Arkansas, for an evaluation. In December 1952 I drove 300 miles to the VA Hospital.

During the evaluation, I eventually ended up interviewing with a psychiatrist. They gave me what is known as an inkblot test. They display various ink blot configurations and ask that you tell them what you see. Confused, I said ink blots. Then I was asked what I saw in the ink blots. Still confused, I again said ink blots. I didn't see any details. Finally, they gave up and showed me what I was supposed to see. I'm not sure what the inkblot test evaluates, but I must have failed.

The doctors decided it must be psychological. I don't believe anyone knew about the BEST eye problem at that time. They were unable to identify my heredity problem. They thought a severe vision problem was perhaps psychological and recommended I return In January 1953 to check into the Psychiatric Ward as a candidate for further evaluation. At 19 years old, I had to take their doctor's recommendation and so I agreed. The question, would I be marked for life as a Psycho?

In January 1953 I checked into the VA hospital at Little Rock, Arkansas, and was assigned to the psychiatric ward. The ward had a barracks-style arrangement with single beds. There were about 15 in the ward. The person next to me was previously a B-26 bomber pilot in WW II and looked the part.

The person across from me volunteered for shock treatment. This procedure involved attaching electrical devices to your head while switching on electricity. Afterward, the person displayed unemotional personality characteristics.

I saw the Psychiatrist three times a week for an hour of discussion. The Psychiatrist was a regular guy about 40 years old and smoked a pipe. He was not one of those nutty Psychiatrists. The hospital treated everyone like a VIP. There were 16 mm movies every night. Because the Korean War was still in progress, several movie starlets, seeking publicity, visited for a photo opportunity with veterans. When the University of Arkansas had a star performer appearing on campus, we were invited and given front-row seats. One of these performers was Ray Charles.

I was asked by the Psychiatrist what I intended to do when I left. I told him I would return to college and study to be an aeronautical engineer. He interjected that maybe I should just plan on being an aircraft mechanic. I thought that was interesting in that I had scored high enough on the Marine Corps examination to qualify for Officer Candidate School. This was confusing. I thought I had scored 100 on a high school I.Q. test. Then I scored high enough in the Marine Corps to go to Officer Candidates School, and now I was told I should aspire to be a mechanic. It seemed that I could score on tests very high or very low depending on the test. I suspect they were all related to how my eyes interpreted what it was I saw. I'm glad that I didn't follow his advice. Who would have believed, that in a few years, I would be meeting with the United States Ambassador to Japan in his Tokyo office?

After three months, while seeing no improvement, the VA stopped my treatment and sent me back to Pittsburgh, Kansas. I had an eye heredity problem and not a psychological problem, but no one knew how to identify the eye defect in 1953. I understand that a vision problem is often associated with psychological issues, but not in my case.

It is a good thing the world wasn't computerized in 1953 because the data would have been easily available for the world to see that I had been in a Psychological Ward. My life could have been a shambles because there would be a black mark in the cloud. Having been in a Psycho Ward could have limited vocational possibilities.

###

Returning to Pittsburg in May 1953, at the age of 20 years old, I dropped by the fraternity house. I met a couple of fraternity brothers who started a conversation about what to do for the summer. We concluded that we should drive to northern California and sign on as lumberjacks and make a fortune. One guy was from Michigan and had an old Chevrolet which he volunteered for transportation as long we drove his car at 50 MPH for the 1,800 miles. He wanted to make sure the motor didn't fall apart.

###

On the first of June 1953, we left for California with each of us having about 50 dollars in our pockets. Our route took us through Dodge City, Kansas where we visited Boot Hill and a saloon where the working girls provided entertainment for the cowboys. We checked the price list for the entertainment. I believe the price was three dollars per customer. The cowboys earned about 30 dollars per month. The town had a population of 15,000, it had little to do or see, so it was a short visit. From there we went over the Rockies and to the Great Salt Lake. Checking out how salty the water was, I accidentally fell into the lake. It was salty, and when my clothes dried, they were as stiff as a board and useless for wear. Despite this mishap it was a great stop. Now onward to Northern California.

###

Finally, late one afternoon, we arrived in a small logging town. Hungry, we went into a tavern for a hamburger and beer. Being strangers in a small town, they were very welcoming until they found out we were looking for logging jobs. That didn't go well. In a few minutes, a large group of loggers came to our table and suggested we leave town immediately. Was that one of the Western challenges, "Get out of Town by Sundown?" Our six shooters were out of ammunition, we didn't contest the challenge. There was high unemployment, and the locals didn't want any outside competition. We took the hint and departed. We had not taken the opportunity to check employment availability with a logging company.

###

With the logging prospects having quickly faded, we decided to drive down to Los Angeles where one guy's uncle was a veterinarian at the Santa Anita horse racetrack. They were delighted to see us and had a great house. We asked for their suggestions on employment, and they gave us some great ideas and invited us to stay a few days.

In 1953, it was easy to get a job, and we were employed immediately. My job was at the Douglas Aircraft assembly plant. I don't remember where my friends were employed. As soon as we all had jobs my friends got a small apartment, and I looked up a close friend that I ran around with in high school. He was living in Los Angeles with his parents and invited me to stay with them for the summer. He was presently working at a bank. After I had gone into the Marines, my friend had been drafted into the Army for two years. Recently discharged, he had returned to Pittsburg and asked a girl to get married. She declined and he moved to Las Angeles where I met him in the Summer of 1953.

###

He arranged a couple of blind dates with bank employees and much to my surprise, he married the same girl that was on our date. I'm not sure how many children they had but he ended up in divorce. In later years, he gave his kids his house. In Los Angeles that was a good deal because house prices were enormous.

###

As for my job at the aircraft plant, I was given a quick orientation and put on the assembly floor. I assumed my task was to learn by experience. My boss gave me several unrelated jobs. It seemed my real task was to run errands for the boss. The only drawback was the six hours of commuting time by bus. There were several bus transfers and while waiting for the next bus the smog caused my eyes to sting. This was a different experience for me than the atmosphere in Kansas. After two weeks, I decided the travel time was too time-consuming. I decided to quit.

###

I was offered a job by a subsidiary of AT&T. After a week's training, I went on the job working in a large building where telephone lines were connected to the various switchboards. We were constantly running wires and soldering hookups. As a new person, it was interesting because I had no idea what was going on except to do what I was told. At one point the boss wanted me to file down a metal bar which served as an electrical ground wire. While filing, the file slipped and accidentally cut through a taped bar, which was the hot wire. Touching them both, with a file, caused a short-circuit of 25 percent of the electrical system. As a result, the telephones connected to that outlet became disconnected.

When a phone became disconnected it would set off a bell. There were several hundred phones disconnected, resulting in several hundred bells ringing. All this caused the disconnection of a large portion to the town's business phones. This caused a massive disruption beyond explanation! Strangely, I was assigned a different job in the building, but amazingly I wasn't fired.

CHAPTER 11.

Home from California in September 1953, at age 20, I returned to college and continued in engineering. It was a normal college year with homecoming parades, fraternity dances, football, and basketball games.

###

The fraternity, looking for additional girls to date, discovered an all-girls college in Nevada, Missouri, a town 45 miles from Pittsburg. I would load up the Frazer on Saturday afternoon with seven fraternity brothers and drive there for blind dates. After four weekends we decided that driving that far, one day a week, wasn't productive. I was still baffled by how I scored on tests. On some tests, I was a Hero and on others a Goat. This is a term used in the cartoon "Peanuts." Being a Goat puts you in the bottom of the competition. Not liking the Goat status, I decided to go to the college testing center and volunteer to be tested on all the tests available. By mid-semester, the testing department had extra time to test walk-in students and were delighted to practice their tests on me. All tests were different, and I took them twice a week. I was doing okay until they gave me a test consisting of Synonyms and Antonyms. I scored in the bottom five percent. With poor reading skill, I couldn't look at a word and imagine the pronunciation. I was unable to break words down by syllables. The testing department was as surprised as I was by the low score. To counter this test, they decided to give me a similar test, with sentences designed to accomplish the same task by placing the individual words in sentences. In this test, I scored in the top five percent

###

For me, the world's greatest invention was "Spell Check" which was developed in the 80's. Spell check became my savior. It would help you spell words, give audio pronunciation and a brief description of its meaning.

###

During this semester, I met a new student who became a lifelong friend. He had just returned from two consecutive years of actual combat in Korea. He started as a tank gunner and worked himself up to the position of company First Sergeant. He headed to college to obtain a commission in the Army through ROTC. He aspired to be a general. After he was commissioned as a Second Lieutenant, he was eventually assigned to the 3rd Armored Division in West Germany. What is interesting is that Elvis Presley was drafted about that time and assigned to the 3rd Armored Division. As it turned out, my friend became Elvis Presley's Platoon Leader and Elvis became his jeep driver. He claimed that Elvis was a good soldier with a pleasant unassuming personality.

This colleague did make Colonel but never General. However, his son was promoted to General, a few years later. Unfortunately, his dad had died two years before he made the promotion.

###

After completing a routine college year, I had to decide what to do in the summer 1954. With no prospect of an adventure, I decided to attend the college summer session and take Physics and a required course in Psychology.

The Physics class turned out to be a fun time. A friend and I decided we needed to liven up the class. We located a large beehive and put several of them in a jar and turned them loose in the classroom. It caused pandemonium and we watched as everyone scattered. We were unaware a bee sting could be fatal to someone allergic to bee stings. We had such a person in the class. Removing the bees took the rest of the class period.

On another day we were in the laboratory studying the amount of electrical energy it took to melt ice. Work in the laboratories is sometimes slow and can become boring. To solve this problem and add a little excitement, we waited until a person had all their wires hooked up and ready to turn on the power. When they threw the switch, we threw ice up their backs. For a second, they thought they had been electrocuted.

It was time for me and my partner to do the experiment. We were convinced this was a simple procedure. We quickly hooked up our wires to the power and threw the switch. In our haste, all the wires were attached to the wrong devices, and we blew out all the fuses on the equipment. That ended the day's activities. At the end of the course, I think the professor would have preferred to give us an "F," because of the unorthodox activities. However, he was a good guy and gave us "A's" based on our test scores. As for Psychology, there was a lot of reading, which I avoided, but still managed a "C," which was passing. All was good. Later I realized that some employers wouldn't even look at your job application if you were in the bottom half of your class.

In the Fall of 1954, I transferred to Wichita University to continue my Aeronautical Engineer Degree. Kansas State Teachers College (KSTC) only provided pre-engineering.

Upon arriving, I needed a little extra money and got a job at the University as an Assistant Custodian. After class, I swept out the classrooms and hallways. After a month I concluded several things. When you transfer you consume a lot of mental energy just learning the culture of the University. Additionally, finding classrooms, methods of study, identifying the professor's personality, and where to live? Unknowingly, this reduces one's capacity to learn resulting in slightly lower grades. If a student is smart, they would arrive on campus during the summer session and take one course while learning the lay of the land.

###

Unaware I was over-extended; I decided to pledge another fraternity and see what they offered in entertainment. A couple of days after enrollment the fraternities decided to have some fun. Early one morning they put up road barriers that directed all traffic into the parking lot. It became a terrific traffic jam. I concluded it's easy to encourage university students to cause mischief. A great tool for creating college campus demonstrations in the 1960's.

###

We had four people in a room in the fraternity house. Most of the athletes joined a competing fraternity, but one did join ours. He was from Pittsburg, and he wanted to be billeted in my room. He had been three years behind me in high school and I didn't know him, but I guess he felt he knew me. I had dated his older sister a few times in high school. Anyway, we became friends.

###

I was slowly drawn into the orbit of football players' activities. They were high-strung and living on the edge, which encouraged them to test the limits of societal norms. They were hard to keep up with and were in all kinds of mischief. If they stepped over the line the "Athletic Alumni Association" in Wichita came to their rescue. I was to be included. Perhaps because I was carefree and enjoyed extemporaneous adventure.

###

We became bored with the slow pace of fraternity life and decided to rent a house. My roommate had become close friends with the star half-back and the three of us rented a house at night. When we saw it in the daylight it was a dump, but we didn't care. The house was a great place for parties and numerous guests dropped by, including several local and college girls. That company was great, but as soon as they found out I wasn't a superhero, they moved on to my roommates.

We must have studied, at some point in time, but I don't remember where or when.

###

We became friends with the owner of a college bar. The owner decided to have my friend tend bar. The purpose was to draw in other college students who were anxious to meet star football players. Many times, the owner would leave for a time and encourage my friends to pass out a few free beers during his absence. It was a great advertisement, and the bar flourished. Running around with these guys led to many adventures that are better to not disclose.

###

Summer of 1955 was approaching when I received a letter in the mail from the Marine Corps. The letter was recruiting Marine Corps college students, with previous active duty, to sign up for three summer months active duty in San Diego. I had been thinking of a military career and this was the perfect opportunity to reacquaint me with the military. As this was happening, a local Cadillac dealer and member of the Athletic Alumni Association asked my two roommates to drive a new Cadillac convertible to California. Included was one of the star basketball players I knew from Pittsburg. They asked me to join them. I did. The dealer covered most of the expenses.

###

Leaving Wichita, we drove straight through to Las Vegas where we stopped overnight at an economic Bed and Breakfast. We quickly unloaded our bags and drove to town. As a 22-year-old, I was amazed by the Las Vegas lights and activity. It was everything that people had bragged about in the news and movies. Las Vegas was much smaller in 1955, but it was big and impressive to me.

###

We drove our Cadillac, with the top down, up to the door of the Dunes casino. We must have appeared, to the doorman, to be high rollers and sons of wealthy parents. The red carpet was rolled out.

You could run into many of the entertainers in the hotel-casino. For example, I saw Jane Powell, a popular movie star who appeared in many musicals.

###

We arrived early in the afternoon, and it wasn't crowded. We decided to play at a "Blackjack" or "21" table. To keep the tables active with excitement they let us win to entice other customers to join in at our table. We felt invincible and on a winning streak. Toward the evening, crowds started arriving and gravitating toward the table of the alleged wealthy boys on a winning streak. With drinks in hand, we were a colorful group bent on breaking the house financially. As large crowds gathered, and the excitement grew other customers enthusiastically began participating in the games. Then as soon as the excitement reached its peak we started losing and were broke in a very short period. Who said casinos were honest? We won until we drew a crowd and then lost. The casino then gave us free drinks for our performance. We did manage to hold onto 20 dollars. No problem, the football players had been given an expense account by the sponsor and they were headed to a highly paid make-believe job being sponsored by the Athletic Association, so they were O.K. The next day they dropped me off at San Diego Marine Recruit Depot. The Marine Corps was now covering my expenses, so I was O.K.

CHAPTER 12.

Arriving at the entry gate of the San Diego Marine Recruit Depot, I disembarked from the Cadillac and walked up to the gate guard with my orders. He directed me to the location of the company that received newly assigned personnel. The company was about one-half mile away and across a huge parade ground. I had a 70-pound duffle bag and asked the guard if there was transportation. This was not a smart question.

He made it abundantly clear, "You're back in the Marine Corps, solve your own problems".

My rude awakening.

I put the duffle bag on my shoulders and trudged to the receiving company.

I expected there to be many ex-Marine college students in attendance, but only five showed up. One of the five had received two Silver Stars during the Korean War while another was from the Rolla School of Mining Engineering.

Leadership at the San Diego Recruit Depot wasn't exactly sure what to do with us, and it seemed they were unaware of the three-month program. Finally, the decision was to send us to Camp Matthews about 15 miles north of San Diego. It was the Marine Corps rifle range, and we were to be Rifle Range Coaches. To prepare for the job, we attended a one-week course and graduated as expert rifle coaches.

###

After a couple of weeks as Rifle Range coaches, the mining engineer student went to the beach one weekend and came back married. When he made the announcement, I remembered back in

1952 when the First Sargent strongly suggested avoiding a weekend marriage.

Two weeks later, he took her to camp to meet the group. Much to my surprise, I knew her from the Pittsburg State Teachers College. We played cards in the student center. This caught the student engineer off guard. What are the chances that a student from Missouri and a student from Kansas would meet on a California beach and we would each other?

In about three weeks, he decided he didn't want to be married. He was a devoted Catholic and that was a problem. He started quizzing me for anything I knew about the girl that would justify a Catholic divorce. I wasn't helpful, I only knew her from playing cards and didn't have any information. I should have tried harder. A few months later, the wife confided in me that her husband had tried to encourage her to jump off a cliff. Now, to me, it would be simpler to change religions.

###

While standing on the rifle range, one afternoon, my vision stress suddenly improved by 80%. I couldn't believe it because this had been a huge problem for the past five years. I still had a reading problem, it seemed like a clamp had been removed from my optic nerve now less distorted vision could flow freely.

###

In August 1955, my three-month period with the Marine Corps ended and I headed back to Wichita University. Enroute, I decided to try for a commission in the military. I had been thinking of this option for some time. Being loyal to the Marine Corps, I had already sent a letter to a university that offered a Marine Officer training program called the Platoon Leaders Course (PLC) program. In the 50's, some military programs had a required 20/20 vision for admission. My question in the letter concerned vision. They responded that the requirement was 20/25 vision, correctable to 20/20. That ruled out the

PLC program for me. I had 20/40 vision, correctable to 20/20, leaving only the Army ROTC as a choice. This was okay with me because the Army had posts around the world and offered a greater opportunity for adventure. Marine Corps assignment locations in the United States and overseas were limited. I had lucked out again, by failing to qualify for the PLC program I could LOOK forward for extensive adventures.

###

Arriving in Wichita, I proceeded to my favorite bar and received a heartwarming welcome from old friends. While hanging out, I began to ponder my financial situation, which didn't take long. I was broke. I had 30 hours or one year remaining to complete an engineering degree. Signing up for ROTC would add 12 hours or another complete semester, leaving one- and one-half years to graduation. Financially, this was not possible.

My G.I. Bill provided one and one-half days tuition for every day of active service. I had been in active service for 16 months and had used up my 24 months, which depleted my G.I. Bill. What to do? The answer was clear, I must return to Pittsburg where I lived three blocks from college and could live at home. Tuition and books amounted to about 80 dollars a semester. However, I would have to change my course of study to business. The common opinion at my college was that the bright students strive to be doctors, lawyers, or engineers. Other less capable students take business courses. Would my ego be okay with becoming a business major?

There really wasn't any choice and I headed back to Pittsburg and KSTC and enrolled in business. Also, I needed approval to enroll in the ROTC program. Prior military service gave you credit for the first two years of ROTC. For the final two years of Advanced ROTC, you had to apply and be accepted. To meet this requirement, you had to take a written examination. So far 60 students have applied, and one-third failed to achieve the required score. Would I be a Hero or Goat when I took the exam? I went over to the ROTC Department and informed them I was here to join. They gave me a disinterested look and said come back tomorrow and take the test. The next day I took the exam, passed, and was accepted. That seemed to be too easy. I'm now a cadet and on track for a commission, which is a big leap from Corporal in the Marine Corps. I had to ask how I scored. The person in charge said I ranked number two in the class. My thought was, how did that happen? There had been synonyms and antonyms on the test, and I was sure that would have been my undoing.

###

Theoretically, I'm in the Army now and needed a discharge from the United States Marine Corps Reserve to join an Army Reserve Unit in town. Joining the Army Reserve Unit required taking another test. This time I scored first in the unit. Maybe this is the right profession for me. There was even a financial upside, I received 40 dollars a month from ROTC and 30 dollars a month from the Army Reserve Unit. Even with this, I still didn't have enough income. For extra money, I applied for a job driving the Pittsburg City Bus for 15 hours a week, which netted another 40 dollars a month. WOW, I'm in the money, $110 a month!

###

It was the day of registration for college years 1955-1956. I walked into the registration area and was assisted by a Professor in the Business Department as my academic counselor. He asked for my form outlining the classes I wanted for the fall semester.

I said, "I didn't have one. I want to sign up for the course of study that would allow me to graduate in two years with ROTC included".

He smiled and said, "I think that's possible; you are in the school of Business with Marketing as your field of interest." Prior rumors were correct, business courses were much easier than engineering courses.

###

As college was restarting, I went over to the Sigma Tau Gamma fraternity to renew my membership. There I met several members of my High School graduation class. They had completed their military enlistment and were returning to college on the G.I. Bill. One of the classmates was President who was running for re-election. He wanted me to run for secretary. That didn't sound like much, but he insisted and explained this was more than a secretary position. I wasn't sure what he was talking about but agreed to be nominated and was elected.

This position as Secretary gave me a seat on the Interfraternity Council, representing the Sigma Tau Gamma. This council was like the United Nations of fraternities. The Panhellenic Council represented the sororities. These councils dealt directly with the Dean of Students on Greek matters concerning the rules of conduct, coordination of athletic areas for intramural sports, dances, rallies, and academic standards. The council also organized the Greeks to vote in a block during the college elections. The goal was to elect as many Greeks as possible and we were successful. The majority of those on the Student Council were Greek.

At the end of the junior year, I was elected President of the Interfraternity Council by fellow council members.

###

In 1955, I started dating a KSTC sophomore from Pittsburg intermittently for the next two years. During this period, she was elected Miss Pittsburg and competed in the Miss Kansas competition. She was an 'A- 'student in language and literature, with Spanish as her major. She played Cello in the orchestra. We were engaged for a brief period, (like a few weeks) because there were obstacles that couldn't be overcome.

I was lucky in avoiding early domestication!

The girl had a vision of being a VIP professor in a secure academic environment. I had visions of adventure and travel, filled with uncertainty. Additionally, the mom didn't approve of me. Years earlier my sister and the daughter had a falling out in junior high and the girl's mom was the one offended. Everyone had forgotten the incident, except for the girl's mother. After graduation, I left for the Army. That was the conclusion of the relationship. Again, I was lucky, becoming domesticated at age 23 or 24 would have been a disaster for future adventures.

At the end of the junior year is a six-week summer camp which was a minimalist version of recruit training, without the intense harassment. The focus was on map reading, weapons, bayonet, rifle marksmanship, and some tactics. Another reason for the camp was to make sure the cadets could adapt to military life.

I departed for ROTC camp, located at Fort Riley, Kansas, in my 1938 Chevrolet, given to me by my granddad. Accompanying me was a high school friend who was the fraternity president. His prior service had been with the 82nd Airborne and a tour in Korea as an Infantryman. I thought camp was simply a pass-or-fail event.

The camp included cadets from midwestern colleges and universities. There were over 1,800 cadets attending camp. Upon arrival all cadets were dispersed. At platoon level, there were 48 cadets, with only one representative from each school. Everyone was a stranger in your platoon.

During training, I found myself being used by instructors to demonstrate the correct positions in bayonet training and marksmanship. This put me out in front of the group, or you could say center stage. Few knew of my prior experience in bayonet training, as well as being a marksmanship coach and a machine gun squad leader in the Marine Corps. No matter, there I was center stage. On the rifle range, I scored high enough to be written up in the hometown newspaper along with three other cadets from KSTC.

At the end of camp, I still thought this was a pass-or-fail event, with a 98 percent pass rate. Then in our platoon barracks, our platoon leader distributed papers to be used or a "Buddy Rating" of your squad of 12 cadets. I had never experienced this before. You had to rate each cadet from 1 to 12. Number 12 being the GOAT. This seemed like a fun exercise if you didn't rate number 12. I had no idea what this test was about. Then we all assembled for a written test on what we had learned at camp. I thought of it as an evaluation of the instruction. There was also another evaluation of you by your Platoon Leader, who was an ROTC instructor from one of the many schools.

Later that day we were assembled, by the Platoon Leader, and he said each person was rated one through forty-eight. To receive the total platoon ranking was a surprise. The evaluation included the written test scores, buddy rating, and the Platoon Leaders evaluation. Then the standings were handed out on individual papers. I wasn't sure I wanted to look. Peeking at the paper, I found I had been rated number one in the "Buddy Rating" and my overall standing was third in the platoon. This put me in the top six percent. That was unbelievable because half my competitors within the platoon were from more prestigious universities in the Midwest such as Notre Dame and Purdue.

I still wasn't aware how the score would be used. Returning to KSTC, I was soon to discover it's importance.

CHAPTER 13.

Back from ROTC summer camp and near the start of the 1956-1957 year, I received a note that the Professor of Military Science (PMS) wanted me to drop by his office. The PMS is the officer in charge of the ROTC program. I was somewhat anxious about the purpose of the visit.

I entered his office and after the customary greetings, "Ron you placed second in the chain of command for the senior year".

This is a surprise.

I responded "Thank you for the confidence"

###

As background, in the first year the cadets are privates, the second-year non-commissioned officers (NCO'S), the third year second lieutenants, and the fourth year you are ranked from 1st Lieutenant through colonel. In the fourth year, the senior cadets run the ROTC Program, except for classroom instruction. My rank was Lieutenant Colonel.

###

After the PMS congratulated me, he continued the conversation, "You are now eligible to apply for a Regular Commission."

I was confused by this statement. I had thought enlisted and the officer system of selection to the Regular or Reserve status was the same. Selection usually refers to the minimum time you would be required to serve on active duty. A regular was committed to a longer term of active-duty service and reserve was a shorter time on active duty followed by hometown reserve meetings. Enlisted could choose either. I thought that was the same for the Officer Corps, but now I'm about to find out from the Professor of Military Science, that this is not true.

The PMS noted my pause and my surprised expression. He continued, “To qualify for selection for Regular Army, the cadet must qualify in four areas. The student must be in the top 10 percent of his ROTC class on campus, in the top 10 percent in summer camp, in the top 50 percent of his college graduating class, be a leader on campus, and receive a recommendation from the PMS. You are eligible in all accounts”.

He went on to explain, “The ROTC Regular Commission was the same commission received by West Point graduates.”

> *Here I am at a small unknown college, eligible to receive a commission equivalent to that of a West Point graduate. This appeared to be the right career choice for me.*

###

The person selected to the top position of Cadet Colonel was my high school friend, fraternity President, and the person who rode with me to summer camp. If there had been a close competition between us for the top position, he had the edge because of combat experience in Korea.

###

During my senior year, I continued attending the Army Reserve meetings which met on Wednesday evening for two hours, rather than one weekend a month required today. After a year with the unit, I was promoted to a three stripe Sergeant. This unit was initially a Military Police Company. It was reorganized after a year into a Signal Company. The night after my promotion and after the meeting, I decided to drop by the fraternity house to show off my new sergeant stripes.

###

The fraternity house was located 50 yards from a popular college diner. Upon arriving, I noticed a group of fraternity brothers in a confrontation with a couple of other students. On closer inspection, I noticed it was with two football players who were also college boxers. A week before I had noticed them in a college tavern. They had been in a bullying mood, and they were trying to entice several of the tavern patrons to throw a punch at them. If they had been successful, this would open the door for them to counter by showing off their boxing skills and sadistically, pound these customers into the ground.

Assessing my fraternity brothers' situation, I decided to intervene. I was wearing my BIG Sargent stripes. Regrettably, my uniform and stripes did not affect the bullies The next thing I knew, I was agreeing to meet them in the boxing ring on campus the following day after school. This diffused the situation, and the boxers went away happy.

###

I had watched a few boxing matches in the Marine Corps to determine who would be the Camp Pendleton boxing champion. The competition was open to all comers and several 19- and 20-year-olds, who considered themselves tough guys, would enter. These young Marines, with little boxing experience, fought in the qualifying rounds. Most were paired with seasoned division boxers, who were working their way to the final match for champion. These novice fighters looked like sparring partners against their well-trained opponents. They would let the kids swing away for a couple of minutes, then throw one knockout punch. It was lights out for the young challengers. Lesson learned, don't climb into the ring with a trained pugilist.

###

The question is, should my ego require me to show up? Not likely, it would be poor judgment to get into an unsupervised boxing ring with trained boxers. I skipped the event with no negative repercussions.

Two weeks later, the leader of the two boxers was playing in a Saturday football game and playing a dirty game, intent on hurting players on the opposing team. The opposing team members became irritated and two of the players trapped him in one of the plays and quickly delivered punishing blows. He was left sprawled out on the football field and was carried away on a stretcher. The referee assessed a penalty, and the game went on. I never saw the boxer again

###

In the Fall of 1956, I was driving a City Bus when a Marine I had known during the summer 1955 boarded. His football team was to play our college that afternoon and he had free time and was able to locate me. He was the catholic Marine who met a KSTC girl on a California beach one weekend and married her. A few weeks later he was trying to get a divorce but needed some derogatory information that would justify his intentions acceptable to the church. At the time, I had no information.

He asked, "Have you come across anything that would help my divorce since I last saw you? I am desperate for any derogatory evidence."

I informed him, "I really didn't know the girl, I just played cards with her. Sorry, I can't help you."

He departed disappointed. Interestingly, I talked to the girl on campus the summer after her marriage. She related to me that shortly after they were married, he had taken her to a cliff above the beach and said, "If you love me you will jump."

The moral of the story is doesn't marry a stranger on a weekend.

###

In the early Fall of 1956, the owner of the bus and cab company died. The company was part of an estate, which was valued at $3000.

This was equivalent to the annual individual wage at that time. The company consisted of four worn-out taxi cabs and four well-used buses

If I were to purchase the company, I would need a reliable maintenance shop. My high school friend, Fraternity President, and Cadet Colonel had a dad with a small maintenance facility. I asked him to join me in the adventure as a partner and his dad could have an exclusive contract for company maintenance. He agreed and we each put up $1,500. When I went to the bank, I was surprised by their willingness to do business. What a difference it makes when you are to be a graduating senior from college with a military commission. Two years earlier I would have had difficulty obtaining a small loan, even with security. Now, with money secured, we own the company.

We immediately made friends with a local gasoline distributor, and he agreed to give us a discount if we bought all our gas through his city distribution point. The taxi cabs were worn out and we needed to purchase new cars. A friend's dad owned the Ford Dealership and agreed to give us a fair discount if we purchased all 4 cabs from them. The final problem was that we had a small office in the center of town that received all calls by landline telephone. When there was a service request, the dispatcher would have to wait for a returning cab to pass the request. We decided to purchase two-way radios for the cabs, eliminating the need for the cabs to return to the dispatch office. Now the taxi cabs didn't have to return to the dispatch office. The driver now receives these calls by radio thus increasing efficiency, productivity, and better customer service.

We now control the city network of internal transportation. I was only age 23.

During my senior year, I had a date with a girl living in the dormitory. In the 50's the curfew in the dorm was 10:00 P.M. on weekdays and 12:00 A.M. on weekends. I picked her up and proceeded to the movies. Afterward, we had over an hour before curfew, and to my surprise, she wanted to visit a small, notorious nightclub that was popular with many college students. It was located down a narrow gravel road three miles from campus.

It was beginning to storm with accompanying intense lightning. There was no traffic, and I stopped to watch the sky's electrical display. As soon as I stopped, a pickup truck appeared from nowhere and skidded to a stop in front of my car, blocking any chance of forward escape. The displaced gravel was flying everywhere pounding my car like huge hail stones. It was a spectacular predicament! A scruffy looking man in overalls, in his late 20's, jumped out of the truck with a shotgun and pointed it at us.

My first speculation was, did I have a date with his girlfriend? He didn't look like a guy she would date. On second thought, she was a college girl, and her family lived in another town.

He was drunk and was staggering toward the car shouting, "I've caught you, cattle thieves!"

He must be thinking, we were conducting an advanced reconnaissance to determine the best location for a cattle truck to load rustled cattle from a nearby field.

Cattle rustling was still a problem in Kansas. My biggest concern was that he was drunk and staggering. If he stumbled, his finger might inadvertently pull the trigger and discharge the shotgun in our direction. He came up to the window looked around and said, "Get out of your car you crook".

He could see I was unarmed.

Several times he got a little close and I thought about attempting to knock the shotgun aside and try to overpower him. If I missed in the attempt, the explosion of the shell would have sent shotgun pellets toward me with a very undesirable ending.

After a few minutes of grumbling, that I couldn't decipher, he began to comprehend that we were not cattle thieves. He slowly began to withdraw, muttering in disappointment that he had failed to capture the cattle rustlers.

On the way back the girl was quiet, and we arrived at the dorm 30 minutes early. As soon as I stopped, she jumped out of the car and sprinted into the dorm.

For some reason she wouldn't speak to me again, even though, I had provided her with the most exciting and unforgettable date in her lifetime.

###

In the Spring of 1957, I won a popularity contest on campus. The contest was labeled "The Cutest Pan (girl) and Ugliest Man." Each organization or club nominated one person to represent them in the competition. I was nominated from my fraternity. Their names and pictures were attached to separate boxes and placed in the Student Union Center and other key locations on campus. In this election, you had to pay to vote. You paid by dropping a penny into the box of your favorite person. At the end of the day, the box with the most pennies won. Somehow, I won and was popular man on campus for a day.

After the awards were presented, I heard a rumor that my fraternity had stuffed the ballot box with extra pennies. If true, that was my first experience with fraudulent elections.

###

It was graduation day at the end of May in 1957. It was also time to be commissioned into the Army as a Regular Officer in the Infantry. My business partner selected a Reserve Commission with 6 months active duty and 8 years in the active Reserves. He planned to return to Pittsburg and continue starting small businesses. While away his parents were to run the Nelson-Damrill Bus and Cab Company. I had visions of returning in 20 years and continuing in small business.

CHAPTER 14.

After graduating college, I left for the Army in July 1957 to attend the Basic Infantry Officer Course at Fort Benning, Georgia. it was 750 miles from Pittsburg, Kansas. I planned to arrive at my destination four hours early., driving an old 1950 green Plymouth Coupe that I had purchased for 200 dollars. I was pushing straight through and at night I would stop for a few short naps in the car. Suddenly, 110 miles from Fort Benning, the car engine began to vibrate, resulting in the shaking and jolting of the entire car. It was running on two of the four cylinders. The valves had ceased to work properly. My speed was slowly, sluggishly dropping. I had just a few hours left before I was required to sign in for duty. I crossed my fingers and kept driving hoping the car would hold together. My last dollar was spent filling the gas tank. There was no money left for repairs or for alternative transportation. The car lumbered along and I arrived at Fort Benning driving at a maximum speed of 25 mph.

###

The four-month course covered all the basic skills required to be a Infantry platoon Leader. Topics included platoon and company tactics, map reading, communications, marksmanship using basic infantry weapons, hand to hand combat and many others. Since we were officers, this was a gentleman's course with limited harassment.

Our living quarters were more like a college dormitory with two officers to a room. There were two beds and a place to hang clothes. It was a modest, plain room. The showers were down the hall. Despite our shoebox quarters, we were delighted to finally be officers.

At one point in our instruction, the school had us do a buddy rating of our squad members of our 12 squad members. You had to rate each officer from one to twelve. Much to my surprise, I rated number one out of the 12, the same had happened to me at ROTC summer camp. I'm not sure what they did with the ratings. My opinion was that this was a study to determine if there was any correlation between this result and future success.

On the rifle range, I came out with the second-highest score in a company out of 200 officers. My Marine Corps time as a rifle marksmanship coach had paid off.

Two months into the course, we had just completed a day in the field and were waiting to be picked up for our ride back to the barracks. Our transportation was 2 ½ ton trucks. Each carried approximately 32 officers. There were fold down seats on both sides of the truck, each seating eight passengers. To add hauling capacity, a two-row wooden bench was placed in the center of the truck with passengers sitting back-to-back and facing outward. We had three trucks in our small convoy. Our driver was about 19 years old; we were number three in the convoy. We boarded the truck in random order as we departed the training area, the lead truck was going too fast, and our driver was left behind.

Our driver took his chance to catch up. We were speeding down a small hill, and our driver used the slope for acceleration to lessen the gap between vehicles. While the driver was speeding to close the distance between vehicles, the convoy had unexpectedly slowed to make a sharp turn at the bottom of the hill. Our driver immediately tried to slow the vehicle on the gravel road, which as slippery as ice. Unable to stop the truck, we went into the turn at an uncontrollable speed, the truck skidded and rolled over. The two of the officers sitting next to me were killed. Sadly, one was to get married that weekend. His fiancé, and both the bride's and groom's families, were in town preparing. We had arbitrarily boarded our truck. I happened to be in the lucky seat. I was knocked unconscious and stayed in a coma for three days with a severe concussion. As I slowly regained consciousness, I saw through the haze, a dozen beautiful, angelic girls.

Am I dreaming that I am Muslim, and these are the promised 40 virgins? Am I in heaven?

As the haze continued to clear, I realized there were about 20 of my fellow officers in the ward. Many had their legs and arms in slings and other orthopedic types of contraptions. Apparently, I had been somewhat unruly while unconscious because I found myself firmly secured in bed. Later, I found out that one of my classmates, named Agar, had an older brother named John Agar who was a B rated movie star in Hollywood. His brother talked to some young movie starlets and models into visiting the wards. This was a great distraction, and everyone seemed to enjoy themselves, even though we were immobile.

"All these gorgeous girls and I can't move.", "Don't worry fellows, we will put our numbers on your casts."

"Wait a minute I don't have a cast. Write your number on my arm."

I smiled as a tall blonde bent over and started to scribble. I was ecstatic until I saw she had drawn a jeep on my arm, she had forgotten the number!

Some officers did get phone numbers written on their casts.

One of the officers who only suffered a broken arm, was killed four months later, in a similar accident while attending Ranger School.

###

After a week in the hospital, I was sent back to my company. I had missed seven days of training and classes. When I returned, they were being tested. Since I had been absent, they told me that I didn't have to take the test, but I did. Being naïve I thought it would be easy. This was my mistake, Since I had missed all the instruction, I didn't score as high as normal, and my overconfidence reduced my class standing.

###

On the weekends I took the opportunity to tour the area near Fort Benning. In the countryside I was surprised to see Black's still living in shacks. I couldn't believe the living conditions because nothing like that existed in Pittsburgh.

Across the river from Fort Benning was Phenix City, Alabama. Up until 1955, it had been one of the most crime-ridden and criminal-infested cities in the United States promoting all areas of vice. In 1955 the city was cleaned up and the movie, "The Phenix City Story," was produced. It demonstrated how the city had been cleaned up. Having recently seen the movie I was determined to visit Phenix City and go to the nightclubs. The clubs seemed to be doing business as usual with burlesque shows and associated activities. That was on the surface, and I had no idea how things were being handled behind the scenes, but the city didn't seem greatly improved.

###

We received our assignments while in the basic officer's course. I was to be assigned to the Infantry School at Fort Benning. That may have been a good assignment, but I wanted an assignment overseas. Reflecting, I enlisted in the USMC in 1951 to go to Korea and ended up in Camp Pendleton. I had joined the military for adventure and travel.

This time, as an officer, I called the officer assignment personnel and requested a reassignment to Europe. As a Second Lieutenant that meant Germany. To my surprise, the assignment branch agreed.

###

Prior to going to Europe, I had volunteered for Ranger and Airborne school. They were to be attended after the basic officer's course which was ending in November 1957. Ranger and Airborne Schools would encompass about five months and delay my assignment until April 1958.

###

After completing the Basic Infantry Officer course in November 1957, I signed in at the Ranger School. The Ranger area was austere and had only the essentials. It looked like a place that could have been close to the front lines in Europe during WW II. The idea of the school was to induce stress like a combat situation.

The stress among the students was extremely high. It was rumored that 50 percent would fail. When reporting for the school they expect you to be in top physical condition. When looking at the other students I could see they were in top shape and prepared for the course. I thought I was in okay shape and had made little preparation. I was just going to walk in and take the class. I figured if you didn't quit you would make it through to graduation.

To my surprise, I failed the PT test on the first day and was shown the door and asked to leave. Not deterred I obtained another set of orders for an earlier Airborne class. Of course, they expect you to be in top physical condition. They required the students to do six pull-ups with your palms facing away. not the normal pull-up with the palms facing toward you. I hadn't attempted this before and was able to do only four. I flunked the PT test and was shown the door again.

###

Having failed the schools, I was now ready to deploy to Germany. I contacted the assignments officer, and they published orders for me to *take three weeks leave and proceed immediately to Berlin.*

How did that happen? Here I am a failure and I'm getting the best assignment in Europe. That was great unconscious timing on my part. Normally, only senior single First Lieutenants were assigned to Berlin. Five of us out of my Basic Infantry Class were assigned and we were to be the only Second Lieutenants in Berlin.

I was on my way to a great adventure.

Before going to Berlin, I went home for three weeks' leave. I took this time to check on the status of the Nelson-Damrill Taxi & Bus Company and visit several friends still in college. I departed Pittsburg the day after Christmas by a small commuter airline that serviced Pittsburg. The aircraft was a WW II, two-engine C-47, that had been reconfigured for civilian use. This was the aircraft that dropped paratroopers in Europe on D-Day. I transferred at Saint Louis, Missouri, and boarded a Lockheed Constellation, a propeller-driven four-engine plane and the first commercial airplane with a pressurized cabin. It was the star of the skies, and I felt like a VIP from a small Kansas town.

We landed at an airport near Fort Dix, New Jersey where I was to board a civilian contracted aircraft for a flight to Frankfurt, Germany. I arrived at 10:00 p.m. and prepared for a flight to Germany the next day. At Fort Dix, I met up with two other classmates who were assigned to Berlin. They were Citadel graduates. Their school was near Charleston, South Carolina and was considered the West Point of the South. They had purposely failed the PT tests of Ranger and Airborne Schools so they could get married before Christmas. They were fortunate to receive orders to Berlin. Oddly, three guys who had failed two schools received the best assignments in Germany. Arriving in Frankfurt, Germany, we began two days of processing, which included an orientation on how to conduct yourself in a politically sensitive area.

CHAPTER 15.

Our military flight took us to Frankfurt, Germany where we stayed a couple of days for processing. One night we went to explore the town; however, it was between Christmas and New Year's, therefore it was a quiet and slow night at most establishments.

###

The Russians had just launched Sputnik and were ahead of the United States in the space race. The waiters, having previously served in the German Army couldn't resist kidding us about how Russia had overtaken the United States, even though we had the advantage of WW II German scientist, Werner von Braun, who had completed his U.S. citizenship in 1955.

I saw three girls at a nearby table and asked the waiter, "Is it alright to ask them to dance?"

I wondered why he gave me the look of, "How dumb can you be?"

"They wouldn't mind," he smirked.

I went over to ask, "May I have this dance?"

One who spoke fluent English agreed, "Of course, I'll dance."

While dancing, I finally realized what the waiter was trying to tell me. They were, 'Ladies of the Evening.'

It was my first experience, and I was overwhelmed with curiosity. The girl was attractive and about my age. She soon realized I had no idea what was going on and could see I wasn't affluent enough to be a good client. Business was slow, and she apparently decided I had enough money to be her escort. She suggested we tour the nightclubs, and I was more than willing. Now she had an evening companion that would give her visibility and a purpose to be at all the key night spots. It was a great education.

Leaving the last club in a taxi, I started to get thoughts of further exploration and education.

As I was considering my options, the taxicab stopped at the first traffic light and another car pulled up behind and blew its horn. She looked back and said it was a customer and she was gone.

###

After such an interesting yet disappointing adventure, I departed the next night at midnight on December 28, 1957, and boarded the train to Berlin travelling through East Germany. A night train ensured we would be unable to observe any activity in the country. We arrived at the border check point about 2:00 A.M. and were told to pull the shades and not to look out of the windows. Of course, everyone peeked. The train was powered by an old steam engine. When you peered through the side of the curtain you could see steam covering the entire check point which was dimly lit and covered with snow. There were several armed Russian soldiers standing guard with their rifles. It looked like a dangerous situation for anyone failing to follow the rules. It was a typical Cold War scene. We arrived the next morning and were invited to several New Year's parties hosted by members of our new organization. I noticed one host had received the "Distinguished Service Cross." He had single handedly destroyed several German Machine Gun positions in WW II. His medal is second only to the "Congressional Medal of Honor." In fact, many of the more prominent officers had been heroic leaders in WW II.

###

West Berlin was like an island, it was a city surrounded by the Russian and East German military. The city itself was divided into four sections occupied by four separate countries: the United States, Russia, France, and England. It was a metropolis with a high level of

International Political intrigue, with more espionage activities than anywhere in the world.

###

When I reported to the Berlin Brigade in December 1957, it was a cold winter day with snow on the ground. It remained heavily overcast for the next 90 days. I noticed I was the only Second Lieutenant in the Battalion of 700 soldiers. My contemporaries were all senior First Lieutenants. That meant I had no seniority and would receive the less desirable tasks and be subject to a fair amount of friendly harassment from my colleagues.

###

My living quarters were outstanding. I had a one-bedroom apartment co-located with other family and bachelor housing near the American military football stadium, the Post Exchange (PX), and the Commissary. These structures were in an upscale German residential area.

###

My schooling completed, I was finally on the job, ready to assume the responsibilities of a Second Lieutenant. In college you are usually required to sit in class, listen to lectures, required to read some chapters, maybe turn in a paper, and participate in a small practical exercise concluded with a written test. Your responsibility is to pass the test. Now you're on a real job, instead of a written test, I saw on the training schedule that I would be overseeing a full day of training in just a few days. That day's exercise will be the platoon in the attack, and you have the entire company of 200 soldiers to train. With little guidance, you're on your own and it's up to you to organize the training. You must develop an hour of instruction and supervise the practical exercise of a platoon of 40 soldiers attacking a simulated enemy position for the rest of the day. In addition to the instruction, you must plan for transportation to the training area, arrange for blank ammunition distribution, and support the needs of the troops.

Of course, all the officers and men are watching in glee. This is your initiation. They are keeping a close watch and will step in if anything starts to go wrong, and a few things did.

One First Lieutenant commented, "How are you going to feed your troops, Lieutenant?

"What do you mean?"

"Where is your mess truck?"

Lesson learned, use your Non-commissioned Officers (NCO's) and delegate authority and responsibility for the accomplishment of the numerous tasks.

###

In the second month of my assignment in February 1958, the command decided to have winter platoon testing. As a new Second Lieutenant, just out of Infantry School, it was a bit of a challenge. I hardly knew the NCO's and soldiers in my platoon. The test consisted of setting up a defensive position, patrolling, and withdrawing, followed by a night attack. I passed but didn't do as well as the seasoned First Lieutenant Platoon Leaders. It was a good test, and now I knew what was expected and immediately started preparing for the next year while conducting several rehearsals. I procured special ammunition and pyrotechnics necessary to do a WOW job. We would conduct a night attack including flares to light the field of action, large firecrackers to immolate live fire, and using whistles for coded control.

Unfortunately, we were not tested again. I know my grand show would have finished first.

The command was reorganizing and had other things to think about.

###

I was now in my third month in country, and it was March 1958 when the command decided to conduct the "Expert Infantry Badge" test. All Officers, NCOs, and Enlisted were required to participate, over 600 personnel in all. The test consisted of numerous individual testing stations and lasted for three days. You would be required to call for artillery fire support, react to a chemical attack, throw grenades at a machine gun nest, hit targets on the rifle range, map navigation, conduct first-aid treatment of wounded, and demonstrate communication skills via radio, messenger, and telephone landline. Each station had to be passed satisfactorily. Failure at any station was automatic elimination. With much effort and my usual luck, I made it through all stations.

Those completing the test satisfactorily were to receive the "Expert Infantry Badge," to be presented at a formal parade with awards pinned on by the Regimental Commander. As I joined the group that was to receive the award, I noticed there were six of us present to receive the honor. Only six completed successfully out of over 600. Fortunately, I was one of the six and received "The Expert Infantry Badge" on that day in March 1958.

###

West Berlin was the location of Spandau Prison. It confined the two remaining ex-leaders of the Nazi Party. The WW II leaders of Germany were put on trial in Nuremberg for war crimes from 1945-1946. Most were executed, three were given life sentences, while some were given 10,15- and 20-year sentences.

Albert Spear and Rudolph Hess were still in Spandau Prison. Albert Spear had received a 20-year sentence and had been Hitler's chief architect and minister for armaments and war production. Rudolph Hess had received a life sentence and had been Deputy Party Leader and for a while named as the second successor to Hitler. In May 1941, Hess flew a Messerschmitt 110 (a two-engine night fighter bomber) to Scotland to supposedly make peace between Germany and England. He was immediately placed in prison in England until the Nuremberg trials in 1945. At the trial, he received a life sentence. Many of the French, British, and American trial lawyers believed he was given an inappropriately, prolonged sentence. They all considered he should have an early release because he was captured too early in the war to commit war crimes. The Russians, who had lost 9 million civilians, would not agree.

The exterior guard for the prison was rotated between the military units of the United States, Russia, France, and England. The interior was controlled by civilians. Military companies, in the Berlin Command, were rotated and periodically were assigned the task. I got one turn as "Officer of the Guard". While in the prison, the civilian in charge gave me a tour of the small prison. He introduced me to Albert Spear. Prisoners weren't allowed to talk to outsiders. Spear nodded his head in acknowledgment of the introduction. He had an impressive presence and radiated a superior level of intelligence. After meeting Spear, we went into the garden, which was used for short exercise and recreation purposes, here we saw Rudolf Hess sitting in the corner on the ground taking constant deep breaths. He had been in prison since 1941 and now was serving a life sentence. He was either doing breathing exercises or had lost some of his mental faculties or was just bored.

These two remaining prisoners were loners and had been the least popular among the previous seven prisoners and their guards. Spears was disliked by his peers for his repudiation of Hitler and his government at the Nuremberg Trial

Hess had an antisocial personality and was considered a hypochondriac, lazy, and perhaps mentally ill. He remained a mystery until at age 93, he committed suicide with the cord of a lamp.

###

I had been in West Berlin for a few weeks and found a social club where soldiers and the local girls met. It was a nice place and had a feeling of a small-town club where everyone spoke English. I noticed that the second floor appeared to be set up for small gatherings. One night the waiter asked me if I would like to go upstairs and join a small party. I was surprised to be invited because I didn't know anyone. I was curious and accepted the invitation. In the small room were several ex-German bomber pilots of World War II, about 10 years older than I was. They eagerly invited me to join in the conversation and everyone was speaking English. Included in the group was an unbelievably good-looking girl.

I would have to say she was more than extremely attractive, and I tried not to stare.

She was escorted by an older woman of about 55. Her chaperone wouldn't let her speak to me and restricted the young woman's conversation to German.

Later, her chaperone left the room for a few seconds.

At which time, she quickly turned to me and in perfect English, "I don't get to meet many Americans."

I responded, "I would be pleased to share a conversation with you. Your English is excellent."

Her escort returned and that was the end of our conversation.

The ex-Luftwaffe pilots said she was a German movie superstar. I thought they were kidding. As the evening went on, the pilots began telling war stories. In one story they expressed their disappointment that Hitler wouldn't authorize their group to bomb London. Their purpose for the mission was to earn the German award of the "Iron Cross." That was the award received for a successful bomb run on London.

###

The next day I was walking in downtown Berlin on Kurfurstendamn, the most famous avenue of Berlin. I walked by a theater and there was the girl's picture on the billboard advertising her as the star of the movie. I never went to the club again. I was busy exploring Berlin. Maybe I should have.

Wishful thinking, I wonder if I could have gotten her number.
theater and there was the girl's picture on the billboard advertising her as the star of the movie. I never went to the club again. I was busy exploring Berlin. Maybe I should have.

Wishful thinking, I wonder if I could have gotten her number.

CHAPTER 16.

In Berlin, the Russian and East German governments were coping with a serious problem. Their engineers, doctors, intellectual scholars, and other professionals were escaping from East Germany to West Berlin because of inadequate border control. This was creating a huge brain drain, until 1961 when Nikita Khrushchev solved this problem by building the 84-mile-long Berlin Wall. This wall was a deterrent to keep East Berliners from escaping. I was assigned there before its construction.

###

Based on international agreements between our allies and Russia, the United States military could travel freely between West and East Berlin. There were checkpoints between the sectors; although, for United States Forces it was just a formality. I traveled unescorted to East Berlin frequently and toured the ruins of Hitler's impenetrable, elegantly appointed 3,000-square-foot bunker. This is where Hitler and Eva Braun committed suicide using cyanide tablets. In addition to the cyanide, Hitler also shot himself. Their bodies were burned outside the bunker and unidentifiable. DNA was not used until 1987. This underground air raid shelter was destroyed and covered up with dirt. Ironically, it's now a parking lot.

As I drove through the city, I observed that approximately fifty percent of East Berlin was still in ruins. The buildings were burned with some bare walls still standing. This was the result of numerous bombings and Russian artillery bombardments during their invasion of Berlin. I noticed, by the rubble of the buildings, that the obvious killing of civilians received little consideration. All Germans were considered the enemy. The Russian leader, Joseph Stalin, insisted that his troops should enter Berlin before the Allies. This plan was considered as desirable by General Dwight Eisenhower, Allied Commander, who wanted to lower his casualties. Stalin wanted revenge for the 27 million Soviet casualties. He also wished to reach Keiser Wilhelm's nuclear research library in Berlin. The price that Stalin paid for his Berlin conquest was over 82,000 Soviets killed in the Battle of Berlin.

###

Continuing my tour of East Berlin, I noticed that the Soviet Union had rebuilt many buildings. The construction was mostly apartment complexes that had been hastily erected and now were in a poor state of repair and looking very shabby.

East Berlin, attempting to present worldwide acclaimed performances hosted performers such as, the English ballerina Margo Fontaine, at the rebuilt Staatsoper (Berlin Opera House). I took the opportunity to attend a few of these performances.

###

On 1 May 1958 (Soviet May Day Celebration), I was selected to escort a military tour bus going into East Berlin. In a somber, mandated celebration, East Berlin workers marched down the main avenues. Strangely, no spectators were watching the formations that stretched from curb to curb, with four or more lanes across. Looking at the faces of the marching workers, they didn't appear very excited about participating in this required activity.

Part of the tour included the Soviet Union Memorial at Treptower Park where 7,000 Russian soldiers are buried, killed during the Berlin fighting.

I never understood why the unnecessary causalities, the war was over, and the city surrounded, and why the Soviets didn't wait for a final truce, instead of getting so many killed. My understanding, it was because Stalin wanted to reduce Berlin to rubble. It was his revenge for the cruelty Germany had caused Russia in their non-compliance with the non-aggression pact of August 1939.

Continuing with our East Berlin bus tour, I instructed the tourists that taking photos was strictly forbidden by the Soviets. The passengers weren't impressed by my firm warning. They snapped away while I deliberately looked away. It was too great a photo opportunity to forego.

###

In the early winter of 1958, I met a lovely brunette girl at one of the clubs who was a hat maker. She agreed to a date, and I was to pick her up at her parent's house on the far edge of Berlin. I am amazed that I found it. When I arrived, I was cordially greeted by her parents who appeared to have been affluent prior to the war. They said they were fortunate to have been able to purchase this small house on an acre of land near the end of WW II. The purpose of the purchase was to move out of the city that had become the target of numerous bombings and later shelling by the Russian Artillery. During my visit, the conversation drifted into events at the close of WW II. Her mother explained that having her seven-year-old daughter present when the Russians passed through, discouraged unwanted advances. The tactic worked, and the Russian soldiers continued to the city.

Another date, she took me to a movie titled 'Stalingrad' which was produced by the German film industry. That battle was one of the worst defeats by the Germans in WW II. I thought it was a very depressing movie, and even more so for the Germans who were viewing the movie with us. I suspect the movie box office attendance was small. Another time, we went to a soccer game at the stadium where Hitler hosted the 1936 Olympics. It was this Olympics that infuriated Hitler because black Jesse Owens, won four Gold Medals in track and field, disproving Hitler's theory of the superiority of the Aerian Race.

###

The early winter months of 1958 were constantly overcast, and there seemed to be not even a slight ray of sunshine. This sometimes led to depression and one of my soldiers committed suicide. He had brought back ammunition from the rifle range and while cleaning his rifle decided to kill himself. He had been a Prisoner of War (POW) in Korea. After that experience, he couldn't handle stress. He wanted to be a Private First Class (PFC) to avoid additional duties. When he was promoted to Corporal, the added responsibility was too much for him. During the same period, the Company Commander in the adjacent company fatally shot himself in the chest.

###

While I was in Berlin, I kept in contact with my business partner in Pittsburg, Kansas. My partner had completed his six months of active duty and returned home to run the taxi-bus company. The business was prospering; therefore, we decided to buy the cab company in Fort Scott, Kansas about 30 miles from Pittsburg. With the successful purchase in Fort Scott, we decided to purchase a third cab company in Oklahoma, 50 miles from Pittsburg. Being too self-assured, we failed to have the books properly checked by an accountant and some problems arose. The most notable problem was that the taxi company was charging only 25 cents per ride. Which was less than the other two companies. The Oklahoma fee didn't cover operational costs. My partner scheduled a meeting with the City Council and asked to restructure the taxi fee. The City Council refused and didn't want their citizens to pay a higher rate. My partner was dumbfounded. The City Council then closed the doors to the public and continued the meeting behind closed doors, giving my partner a detailed explanation of how they envisioned the taxi company should operate. The council explained this was a DRY County. This meant no alcohol could be sold legally. The city residents weren't happy with the situation and the Council wanted to solve this problem. Their solution for the citizens and the taxi company was that the company was to make money by delivering alcohol to its citizens. The taxis were to go across the county line, where purchases were legal, obtain the alcohol, then drive back across the county line and deliver to customers. This is bootlegging and highly illegal. The Council wanted an informal agreement. No written contract would be made. My partner and I considered this proposition too risky. He abandoned the company in Oklahoma, took a financial loss, and departed the town.

In Pittsburg more difficulties arose, a customer caught their finger in a closing taxi door and decided to sue. My partner decided he would go to Law School so he could handle these kinds of cases. We departed for law school in Topeka, Kansas, and left the business with his parents to run. I remained a distant financial partner.

###

During this same period, the ammunition plant where my mom was employed in Parsons, Kansas closed. She considered this an opportunity to return to college at age 47 and become a teacher. For finances, she was still drawing Social Security as a widow, and it would continue until my 14-year-old sister turned 18. In addition, I was able to provide 50 percent of her support and declared her a dependent. As a dependent, she receives my housing allowance. I was not required to pay for my Bachelor Officer Quarters because I was separated from my dependents. This was an excellent arrangement. This funded my mother's college education.

###

Back in Berlin, I participated in an exercise on how to handle captured prisoners. To make it realistic, a few members of the company were designated prisoners. They thoroughly enjoyed that assigned role. Their goal was to escape by any means possible. They were not restricted by any rules. One prisoner, using his ingenuity, broke loose. Instead of escaping, he headed straight for me.

In the Marine Corps they teach you how to use a rifle as a lethal weapon without discharging it. Being a new Second Lieutenant I was the target. As a matter of reflex, I grabbed my M-2 Carbine rifle. He was attacking and I was challenged to respond. As he approached, he was in line for a perfect butt stroke to the head. This was my involuntary reaction. If I hit him, it could have cracked his skull and killed him. At the last moment, a mysterious force stopped me from striking his head, allowing the soldier to tackle me. We rolled to the ground. He wasn't very strong, and I easily subdued him. He didn't mind the scuffle because he had successfully tackled a Second Lieutenant. He went back to the group of simulated prisoners as a hero.

"Why did you hesitate with your rifle?' he stated.

"I didn't want to clean gray matter off my rifle."

###

An additional task, as a Second Lieutenant, I was to periodically be assigned to serve as the Officer of the Guard. The job was to provide security of our military compound after duty hours. Twenty soldiers were assigned to assist. This was my initial experience. I had been in the unit for two months. The task for the guard was to control the gates and provide security with a roving patrol. The compound was generally quiet with little external threat expected. The main job was to check soldiers into and off post. The few rules were that soldiers leaving the post had to be dressed in a coat and tie and unmarried enlisted and NCOs had to return to the compound by midnight.

On my first night, a single Senior NCO stayed out past curfew. He was highly intoxicated from his exploits on the town and was aware that if he went through the gate he would be put on report and receive some form of disciplinary action. To avoid this consequence, he decided to avoid the gate and climb over the wall. However, my alert roving patrols saw and captured him at 2:00 a.m. The guards brought him to the guardhouse. The NCO requested to use the restroom. From the lavatory, we heard a loud crash of a window being broken. We rushed to the bathroom and found the NCO had crashed through the window and escaped. We ran out of the guard house in pursuit.

We saw him running through the dark and he disappeared. In a few seconds, his shadow suddenly reappeared. I drew my Colt 45 pistol, and laid down on the ground to silhouette him against the background, just like my training had instructed me in the Marine Corps. I had him in my sites, but the pistol wouldn't fire. The pistol, fortunately, for him and me, jammed. In the adrenalin of the moment, I could have ruined my career and possibly killed him. Of course, shooting at an NCO is NOT a proper reaction in this circumstance. In reality. hitting a moving distance target at night, with a pistol, is impossible.

He disappeared again into the dark. Then we heard an agonizing scream ahead of us. Investigating, we found the NCO tangled in six feet high concertina barb wire. Concertina wire is a type of barbed wire, razor-sharp, that is formed in coils that can be expanded like a concertina. The coils are approximately three feet in diameter. This type of wire can be used as a barrier around a defensive position. Usually, two rolls serve as the base with the third role stacked on top resulting in a six-foot wire barrier. The wire he ran into was being utilized for a class on how to protect a defensive position.

"Dammit, get me out of this!"

"Do you surrender?" we all chuckled.

The NCO was cut up by the wire; we called for an ambulance. A few days later, he was given a Special Court-Martial and lost a stripe.

Guard duty is usually non-eventful, so this was a special night. A young officer and his enthusiastic soldiers had made a capture.

I had almost cracked the skull of one junior soldier and nearly shot an NCO. My personal lucky protector was working overtime. What can happen next?

CHAPTER 17.

In the summer 1958, we traveled by steam train to Grafenwoehr, West Germany for six weeks of training in a field environment. Grafenwoehr Training Area is the largest in Europe and was used by both the United States military and the German military. The weather was exceptionally cold for June and July.

###

Training responsibilities were rotated between the officers, and I was accountable for the training every four days. A couple of days, before one of my exercises, I decided to make a reconnaissance of the area with my jeep and driver. I didn't think about checking with Range Control to see if the area was in use. When I arrived at the location, it was late afternoon and most training had been completed. It looked vacant and I didn't see any red flags that designated the area was in use. The surrounding areas also appeared unoccupied. We drove our jeep onto the range and to the top of the hill that was to be the objective of our live fire (real bullets) field exercise, of a company in the attack. It We had a great view of the terrain, and it was easy to see how the plan of an assault should be conducted. As I was standing there, I started hearing rifle fire. I begin hearing bullets ricocheting off rocks a few yards down the hill, with the spent bullets bussing through the air and landing very close. I looked down the hill and a German Infantry Unit was attacking the hill with live fire ammunition. This got my attention. I started blowing my jeep's horn. Jeep horns are not very loud and couldn't be heard over the rifle fire. I became concerned as the Germans moved closer and closer. After all, we were standing on their objective. We were an unattended target.

The driver and I looked at each other, "Sir, I think we should leave." I could only respond, "Affirmative!"

They finally saw us or heard the horn and ceased firing. The driver promptly started the engine, skidding down the steep hill. We left immediately without an introduction or explanation.

I'll bet my driver told some tall tales and whoppers that night.

###

After six weeks in the woods, we returned to Berlin. Several of the single officers and I decided to celebrate and go to a popular ballroom/nightclub. The club featured a large band with an attractive singer who was billed as the top Berlin entertainer. At intermission, there was a sensational water show on the stage. Customers sat at large numbered tables that were equipped with an air tube for sending written messages by capsule to other tables. All messages were screened for appropriateness. If you saw a girl that you were interested in at another table, you could send her a message and ask her to dance. If she agreed, you received a return message or maybe she would wave in acknowledgement.

We soon discovered you could purchase a bottle of cognac for the same price as wine. Cognac was sipped slowly and lasted a lot longer. After a few cognacs, we started having a good time. I was watching the attractive singer and decided to send an air tube message asking her to meet with me at intermission. I didn't expect a response. Within 10 minutes I heard the swish of a message arriving via the air tube. To our amazement, she agreed and came over to the table during the water show.

We introduced ourselves as army officers stationed in Berlin. She was impressed and agreed to go on a date with me. I believe the primary reason for her amiable acceptance to my offer is that she needed a suitable escort, and I could afford to take her to expensive places. The exchange rate was four marks to one dollar. United States military was popular in West Berlin because our presence kept the Russians out.

There were approximately 100 single American officers in West Berlin, making us unique. On a date, she could have a legitimate reason for visiting nightclubs where she could talk to performing contemporaries and maintain visibility in the entertainment business, while on the arm of an officer. As her escort, I was included in many of the after-closing hour parties. There was a lot of underlying stress at these events. It seemed the performers were in continuous competition among themselves to get top billing.

One night, when leaving a club, there were half a dozen tough-looking, teen-age hoodlums partly blocking the entrance/exit, attempting to start a confrontation. When they saw I was an American, the insults commenced. Things looked threatening and I thought we would be assaulted at any second. In a conflict, one on one, you have a chance to be victorious. If there is more than one your chances diminish exponentially.

I thought my goose was cooked.

In my opinion, there was only one thing to do. I put on a poker face, ignored them, and avoided eye contact. Surprisingly, we made it to the car and got in without an issue.

I could see my date was visibly shaken. I felt she must have thought I was a wimp for not standing up to the hoodlums.

Instead, she surprised me by saying, "You handled that situation amazingly. There have been many teenage gangs since the war. They can be dangerous."

My restrained response was, "These kids were just stunned by such a pretty lady."

###

At the end of the summer of 1958, I received a set of new orders, outlining another additional duty. As a Second Lieutenant, I was to serve as the Army's version of a "military lawyer" in a Special Court-Martial Trial. At the Regimental level, an Army officer served in this capacity. My job was Trial Counsel (prosecutor), and my first case was in two weeks.

###

There are three levels of military justice. The first level is the Summary Court which is conducted by a Captain or higher-ranking officer who is both judge and jury. A Battalion commander can convene a Summary Court. The maximum punishment for junior ranks can be one-month confinement or hard labor for 45 days. All lower ranks and NCO's can receive two months restriction to a designated area, forfeiture of two-thirds of one month's pay, and reduction in rank.

The second level of military justice is the Special Courts Martial, which and in the late 1950's, consisted of a Trial Counsel (prosecutor), Defense Counsel, and a panel (jury) of at least three officers. The trial Counsel is usually junior to the Defense Counsel. The senior officer on the panel serves as the judge. This court can be convened by the Regimental Commander and the officers on the court are from the Regiment. It's considered an internal affair. An accused enlisted soldier can require that one-third of the court be enlisted. The maximum punishment could be six months confinement, forfeiture of pay for six months, and a reduction in rank. This is the punishment as I remember it. Today this court is conducted by military lawyers of the Judge Advocate General (JAG) and the punishment has been slightly changed.

The third, and final, military justice level is the General Courts Martial and can be convened by the Division Commander or, in this case, the Berlin Brigade Commander. The maximum penalty is the DEATH SENTENCE. This court will be discussed later in the book as I become more involved with General Court Martials.

###

The longest and most controversial of Court Martials was that of Brigadier General (BG)Billy Mitchell in 1925, who was found guilty of the vague charges of "Insubordination and conduct of a nature to bring discredit upon the military service." BG Billy Mitchell demanded that air power be required for future national security. He accused his superiors, of being "guilty of the criminal offense of treason, incompetence, and negligent." BG Mitchell resigned rather than be disciplined for outspokenly asserting there must be an Air Force"

###

For now, I'm going to court in two weeks. I quickly located a copy of the "Uniform Code of Military Justice," which is several hundred pages, and started scanning it to determine my responsibilities. This was my crash course for Army justice.

###

Fortunately, I won all my cases as Trial Counsel. It wasn't that hard because the commander made sure he had the evidence for a conviction. The Defense Counsel's main job, after the conviction, was to attempt to obtain a reduced sentence.

An example of one case I tried as about a soldier who was charged with dealing in the Black Market. Many items sold in the Commissary and Post Exchange (PX) were either unavailable in the German economy or much cheaper at the PX. Remember, the four-for-one money exchange rate existed at that time. Items of interest were alcohol, clothing, specialty food items, and especially gasoline coupons.

I almost got tripped up on the gasoline coupons myself. A fellow Lieutenant, one evening, while we were playing a friendly game of BINGO in the Officers Club, asked to borrow a couple of gas coupons. He said he was completely out of gasoline. Naively, I handed him a couple of coupons. The next day, at the Court Martial I remembered he was the Defense Counsel for the soldier on trial for black marketing. Of course, he stated my illicit exchange of coupons. I was so startled by his deceit that I laughed and so did the jury. It was perceived as a joke, except to the red-faced receptionist.

###

A few months later, I was promoted to First Lieutenant and was assigned as a member of the court panel or jury. The senior officer serves as a judge and panel member. During my first court hearing, the Defense Council can challenge court members and have them dismissed. This was my first experience as panel member, and while I was sitting there, I noticed all the senior panel members were being systematically challenged and dismissed, leaving me as the judge. The Defense Counsel knew I had no prior experience on the panel and his game plan was for me to fumble as judge. Fortunately, I had extensive experience as a Trial Counsel and was very familiar with the "Code of Military Justice." Much to my surprise, I had mystical recall of the code, and the trial was concluded in a satisfactory manner. After a couple of more trials, this additional duty was passed on to the next officer on the roster.

###

In November 1958 Nikita Khrushchev, Soviet Premier, demanded that the United States, Britain, and France depart Berlin in six months. Was this political saber rattling or was the 'Cold War' heating up? This rhetoric made President Eisenhower anxious. No worries for me, Bob Hope was coming to Berlin to produce his upcoming annual Christmas TV show, and I was able to obtain a ticket.

This was a different type of show. It was being taped for TV and they wanted everything to happen as planned in the script. If the timing was off, they would do a retake two or three times. All in all, it was good entertainment, and on the upside, you were able to see the show several times. Entertainers in Bob Hope's USO show troop were Les Brown and his Band of Renown, Gina Lollobrigida, Hedda Harper, Jerry Colonna and Miss World. Bob Hope continued his USO Christmas shows overseas, often in war zones, for 40 years. If you happened to see the Bob Hope's 1958 TV Christmas Show, I was there. After the show had left town, the Generals commented that Bob Hope's 'chain of command' was much more responsive and authoritarian than the army's due order.

###

One of the single Lieutenants in the Berlin Brigade was First Lieutenant Schwarzkopf, who later became a four four-star general and commanded the troops during Desert Storm in the first Iraq War. I occasionally bumped into him at a few socials. If he knew me, it would be because I was one of a few Second Lieutenants in the Command. I knew his name because he already had a very positive reputation and all his contemporaries spoke highly of him. During his tour, he became the Aide to the Commanding General of Berlin. I met him twice after that. I will discuss these meetings later in the book.

CHAPTER 18.

In January 1959 I was promoted to First Lieutenant. I was no longer the only Second Lieutenant in the Battalion. A battalion had four companies and about 600 soldiers. I had been in the unit for one year and was to receive my first efficiency report (report card) by the Company Commander. He was a true combat leader and had won the Silver Star in Korea by destroying an enemy tank. The Silver Star is the third-highest award for bravery in combat. He praised my outstanding report, presenting a big show of it by having slide rules and calculators. He pretended it was a complex procedure to write a report. I believe, all this was for my entertainment. An efficiency report is simple to write. After all the fanfare, the commander concluded by assigning me to be the Platoon Leader of the Weapons Platoon ahead of more senior Lieutenants. This assignment is important because I now have my own jeep., and I ride instead of walk. The platoon has three 81mm mortars and each mortar has its own ¾ ton truck. Additionally, there are Two 106mm recoilless rifles (anti-tank guns), each mounted on a jeep. I had a fleet of six vehicles that had battlefield mobility, with power not to be ignored.

This was the reason for celebration, as I was one year in the company, then promoted and assigned to the Weapons Platoon. What's more, I was given seven days R & R (Rest and Relaxation) leave to Garnish, Germany. Garnish in the Bavarian Alps and includes the Zugspitze Mountain which is 2,962 meters above sea level. The Army had a Recreation Center with excellent snow skiing. A couple of days later I departed at dusk for Garmish, Germany by car. Military could travel by, train, bus, or car from West Berlin through East Germany to West Germany. Driving by car, you transit East Germany and are required to stop at a Soviet checkpoint at the edge of town. Your papers are checked, and you are given a pass to proceed. The pass was stamped with the time of departure and the time of the required arrival at the West German checkpoint. They allocated just enough hours to arrive in West Germany. If you took longer, you could be detained in East Germany on the assumption, you were spying. At Garnish, I got my first view of the snow-covered peaks of the Swiss Alps.

This is hard to believe, a boy from the vast plains of Kansas getting my initial glimpse of the magnificent Alps.

First on my agenda was to learn how to snow ski. I rented ski equipment, headed to the beginner slope, and started teaching myself the sport. After several falls, I progressed to the point where I could ski down the less challenging slopes. At the restaurant at the bottom of the slopes, I shared hot chocolate and rum apple cider in front of a crackling fireplace with several girls. However, as soon as they found out I was a novice skier, they vanished.

I purchased tickets to ride a cable gondola that transported me high into the mountains offering an unbelievable view. My seven days passed quickly.

###

Returning to Berlin, I had to travel through East Germany again at night. In the dark, I misread a road sign and turned right at an intersection instead of going straight ahead. I was traveling deep into East Germany and off the designated route. After about 10 miles I was suddenly surrounded by red flashing lights and loud sirens of vehicles in front of me, blocking the road two vehicles coming up behind me. These were the autobahn polizel. (German highway patrol). I wasn't sure what was going on, but knew I was getting a lot of attention. I pulled over and they began searching me and the vehicle. By this time, I had figured out I was on the wrong road.

I thought I was going to be a political prisoner and charged with spying. On the upside, I could see myself in all the news media as the latest American held for spying. That would be impressive in our small Pittsburg, Kansas newspaper reporting that the owner of the city Cab and Bus Company was being held as a Soviet spy.

After a while, the police motioned for me to get into my car and follow them.

I could hear the prison doors clanging behind me.

Instead, they escorted me back to the intersection and sent me on my way. After imagining I would be the topic of international news, I was both disappointed and relieved. I was not arrested; however, I had missed my opportunity for notoriety,

###

The holidays were over, and our military and political leaders were assessing the Soviet's mandate that the United States and its allies must depart Berlin in May 1959. A new defensive plan was developed for the city. My company's mission was to assist in the defense of Tempelhof Airfield. In preparation, we made a physical reconnaissance and determined how quickly we could move to and occupy our positions if war was declared.

My weapons' position, for my two 106mm recoilless rifles, was on top of the roof of Tempelhof Airport. These weapons each weigh about 500 pounds. They can be broken down into smaller pieces for movement into a static position, they are still heavy and difficult to move. The building's roof provided a great view of the area and streets below. Enemy tanks would be in full view and easy to engage. There was one problem. These weapons were to be mounted on a tripod. For it to have no recoil (no kick back), an equal amount of energy had to come out of both the front and back simultaneously. When fired, the 32-pound shell created a tremendous back blast in the form of a huge fireball accompanied with smoke. The weapon would light up the sky and the enemy could easily identify your position. Stationary, on top of a building, and unable to move quickly, the anti-tank weapon would immediately draw return fire from the enemy tanks. With luck, one or two shots could be fired, before the crew would have to abandon their weapon and sprint from the area to avoid being disintegrated by incoming enemy fire. That's why the weapon is generally mounted on a jeep. After firing a couple rounds you can quickly move the jeep to another firing position. While I was considering what actions should be taken when receiving incoming fire, I remembered a story about positioning and incoming fire that my granddad told me about from

WW I.

###

One Saturday evening my grandfather, who operated a steam shovel for strip mining coal in the Pittsburg area, and his friend, the owner of a vehicle repair shop, were drinking beer on his large front porch. I sat down on the steps to listen to their conversation and share the cool breeze. I was eleven years old, and WW II was raging.

After a few drinks, they were more relaxed and started talking about their WW I experience.

My grandad's friend stated to me, "Your grandad and I were assigned to an Artillery Battery in France during WW I. Each of our six guns had a ten-man crew, with six horses to move each cannon. When our artillery fired on the enemy, the Germans would detect the firing position and would return fire to destroy our firing Battery. One day our position was pinpointed. We began receiving massive fire from the dreaded German Big Bertha howitzer. Bertha's blasts were digging holes all around us. We were greatly outgunned. A barrage of artillery fire landed on our position, killing some of the horses and destroying our artillery piece. After the shells landed, instinctively, I started running from the impact area, thinking I was escaping to safety. Your grandad saw what I was doing and grabbing me by my web gear he dragged me into one of the newly created shell holes. I was puzzled."

Your granddad quickly reminded me, "once a position is fired on, the fire is shifted to engage a fresh target."

"I looked up and saw the guns had shifted and were firing on the position I was attempting to escape. I was fortunate, your grandfather saved my life that day."

My grandfather wasn't going to let that story go without comment, "You weren't that lucky, you received a shrapnel wound to the skull, the next week, during a similar encounter. Show my grandson where the silver plate is in your head."

I reluctantly touched the area.

I realized Granddad was a hero.

###

So much for reminiscing, back to my job of dealing with tanks and probably some artillery fire. With Soviet spies watching, the United States made a deliberate show of our intentions to defend the city and resolve to stay under any circumstances. Khrushchev, facing this determination, later published in his biography, that this conflict would cause unacceptable casualties on both sides.

###

In February 1959, I ran into a German model at a social event. I'm not sure where she came from, but there she was on my arm.

"Hello, I visit Berlin every winter to see my mom. The rest of the year I work in the States. I would like to show you around."

Later, she said she was a model. It was a good story, and I wasn't interested in its validity. She certainly looked the part.

###

One sunny afternoon, she invited me to a family gathering in a rural section of the city. When we arrived, I noticed a couple of the family members fought in WW II. Later that day, I learned they had fought on the American front in the Infantry. They were polite but you could tell, by their facial expressions, I was still considered the enemy. They weren't sure if they should be cordial or distant. Naturally, they thought they should have won.

An hour went by, and they couldn't resist the temptation to talk about my Buick, "I like your American car and I've never ridden in one. How does it ride?"

I determined they wanted to ride in the Buick, so I did one better.

I tossed the keys to them, "Why don't you take it and see for yourselves how it drives? I'll be here all afternoon, so take your time."

They came back an hour later delighted. "Danke, it has a lot of power and goes fast. All my friends enjoyed the ride."

"Anytime. I should be back."

I was accepted.

###

On a later date, my model showed up wearing a mink coat with a camera slung over her shoulder. Both items were unusual for Berlin.

She said in a burst of bravado, "She asked, can you take my picture?"

"Sure."

"She continued, Could you take my picture modeling in front the old Reichstag building? (Parliament Building in 1933)."

What, that's in East Berlin!"

"I know, my magazine would pay a lot for such a rare picture."

At the time, I was thinking that, of course, we could go to East Berlin. I had driven there several times before.

"Sure, let's go. We're on our way"

###

United States military personnel cars had a special license plate which allowed us to drive between East and West Berlin. The guards on both sides would look at your license plate and wave you through. The guards could stop you and ask for more identification if they felt there was justification. We passed into East Berlin and proceeded on our photo shoot. A West Berliner being photographed in East Berlin was unusual. She was having a good time being photographed in a restricted zone and after an hour it dawned on her what she had done. Would she be able to get back? She turned pale, felt nauseous, and looked anxious.

It was a nice sunny afternoon when we arrived at the East Berlin gate. The guards on both sides were enjoying the weather and somewhat lax in the performance of their duties. The East Berlin guards were busy talking when we arrived at the gate, and slowly one left the group to wave us through. We didn't look like a normal American couple. The guard paused, and looked, but did not wave us through. He was looking at her very carefully.

Then a look came over his face as if he was thinking**,** *this was going to be too much trouble***,** he reluctantly waved us through and returned to the conversation with the other guards. As expected, we had no problem on the West Berlin side of the checkpoint. If caught, she could have been imprisoned by the East Germans for a long time., I could have been court-martialed for smuggling a German across the border. We were lucky that day.

After that adventure, she disappeared for a couple of months. Then she called and said she was returning to the United States and asked if I would see her off at the bus station. There were no commercial airlines in West Berlin, and everyone had to go to Frankfurt for international flights. She was there with her mother, and she gave me the address of her married sister in Georgia so we could communicate. Then both departed for Frankfurt. We did exchange one letter, after I returned to the United States, but she was on the east coast, and I was on the west coast. That was the last of our international intrigue.

CHAPTER 19.

In February 1959, the company was assigned a new Company Commander and Executive Officer. The previous commander was a combat veteran and looked the part. Combat veterans are more flexible because they have experienced the uncertainty of an ever-changing battlefield. The new Company Commander appeared to be an administrator with little flexibility.

###

In my second year, replacements were married and just regular everyday domesticated officers. Fortunately, our new Executive Officer was single. We had a great time every night looking for new adventures. I don't think our conservative Company Commander was overly excited with the Executive Officer and me in our off-duty exploits.

The new Executive officer was a West Point graduate, a Russian linguist, and had been on the boxing team at West Point. He had the profile of an 1890s boxer. Before his arrival, he had been a translator at Potsdam, which was located on the outskirts of Berlin.

###

Potsdam had been where WW II leaders (Truman, Churchill, and Stalin) met to discuss the future of Germany in July 1945. In the 1950's it was used by allied officers, who were authorized to travel throughout East Germany to ensure post-war agreements were being followed. The Russians were authorized to do the same in West Germany and ran their operation closer to West Germany.

###

This new Lieutenant had been reassigned from the prestigious post at Potsdam because of an incident. He had been dating a German waitress at Potsdam who was also a university student in Berlin. He had a drinking problem. The girl who he was dating was extremely attractive and was from a prominent German family. After a few dates, she decided not to see him again. However, he was determined to see her and after a few drinks decided to go to her house. No one would answer the front door. He jumped over the stone fence to try the back door. Waiting for him were two German shepherd dogs. The dogs didn't like the intruder's presence and became hostile. Fortunately, the parents were home and able to call off the dogs before much damage was done. On the downside, this incident resulted in a police action. As a result, the Officer was relieved of his duties in Potsdam and assigned to our company.

###

He and I hit it off immediately and we started touring the town looking for adventure. We had a list of the off-limits Berlin establishments. We were curious and decided to check them out to see how they got their reputations. The military police would check them periodically by coming into a club and quickly look around for any Americans. We happened to be present one night when they were making their rounds.

A sympathetic bartender alerted us, "You men are Americans soldiers, right?"

"Yes, we are. Is there a problem?"

"The MPs just pulled up out in front."

"Where can we hide? Maybe sneak back door?"

"Kein (no), you don't have time. They're coming in now. Step behind the curtain."

He went to the nearby stage and lifted the red velvet drape.

We had no choice but to comply, they were already walking around in the front room.

We heard one MP questioning the bartender, "Any American soldiers here, it's off limits, you know?"

"Look around for yourself!"

"Call us if any show up, *Danke.*"

The curtains hadn't been cleaned for a while, the dust whirled into our nostrils, but we held our sneeze until we heard their departing footsteps and the closing of the entrance door. We waited for the jeep to depart.

It appeared some places put themselves off limits to foreign soldiers and preferred serving only German customers.

We had been courteous and had increased their business, so they had no objections to our patronage.

Eventually, our pursuit of the off-limits taverns lost its exhilaration because we had visited most of them with little excitement.

###

One night the Executive Officer decided to show off his linguist skills and started speaking Russian. This drew immediate hostile looks by the waiter and the patrons nearby.

What was the problem?

We were having a good time and continued. Finally, the waiter grew tired of our activities and approached the table with a stern face.

"Do you realize that the Russians had recently killed thousands of Berliners' and occupied the city. We don't like anything Russian, including their language."

We were embarrassed and took the waiters hint and left the establishment.

###

When first assigned to Berlin, most of the Lieutenants were single and the commanders were heroic officers from WW II and Korea. In my company, all the lieutenants were single and led interesting lives. One Lieutenant played football on the Berlin team and was absent half of the year participating. Military bases had their own football teams and stadiums in the 50's. His dad was a banker on Wall Street and insisted his son finish with football, the military commitment and return home to a 'real profession' on Wall Street. Also, his girl wouldn't marry him until he settled down in New York.

The next lieutenant was a judo expert and marksman. He spent most of his time at shooting matches.

A third lieutenant spent his early evenings in the gym and later became a Chinese linguist. He was selected to escort a USO show and married one of the performers. When he returned, the company had a new commander, and he didn't think the new commander would be a competent leader in combat. I agreed he was more of an administrator than a leader.

To my surprise, one day he asked me, "If we get into a serious conflict, will you back me up in taking over the company? If not, we will all be killed!"

That would be considered mutiny.

"I agree, however, I remember an incident in WW I, that my granddad, who was in the artillery in WW I, told me about how in May 1917, an entire French 2nd Infantry Division refused orders for a suicidal frontal attack that they saw as futile. Both the French and German soldiers were in trenches facing each other. To come out of the trenches (go over the top) and expose yourself was suicidal. Both sides covered the open area between trenches with intense machinegun fire. It had been tried several times unsuccessfully, and with high casualties. They had no confidence in their Commander, General Robert Nievelle. This mutiny spread throughout the French Army. The men did not overthrow their officers and continued to protect their defensive position; they simply would not attack. The results were that General Nievelle was relieved of command, and numerous arrests followed with 3,427 court martials. There were 2,878 sentenced to hard labor and 629 were sentenced to the death penalty of which 49 were carried out."

I hope this narration will give him second thoughts about our mutiny.

If he was serious, it wouldn't have mattered whether I said yes or no, since we were outnumbered and would have been quickly killed or captured before he could have executed his plan. Fortunately, this conflict didn't occur. This mutinous plot was never mentioned again.

###

By June 1959, the Soviet threat that the United States and its allies leave Berlin by May 1959 had come and gone without incident. With no war imminent, the command decided we should continue with our annual summer trip to West Germany for field training, with one change, this year's training was limited to three weeks and was to be conducted at the Hoeffel Training Center. Both the move and training were routine.

###

In Berlin, we had British and French counterparts, and we attended each other's social gatherings. The British representative was a young single officer. British Officers were forbidden to get married until they turned 25. We would invite the British officer to accompany us in the evening. One night we took him to the club that had the water show during intermission. We were having a good time drinking cognac. The British officer had too many drinks and was becoming unpredictable. While we were busy talking to the girls, we didn't notice he had left. We weren't concerned and expected him to return shortly. To our surprise he didn't return. We later learned, from other British Officers, he had decided to go backstage, during the water show. He was caught in a puddle of water attempting to adjust the valves. This action led to his quiet apprehension. He was turned over to British authorities, who frowned on such conduct. As punishment, the officer was returned to England the next day. We suspect he may have had other incidents. British soldiers often referred to Berlin as a punishment post because of the opportunity to get into off-duty mischief.

###

Our French counterpart was a captain with a mixed ethnic background. He had a company in Algiers and had lost most of his men in combat. He appeared to be in an unfavorable status, because of the past, and was attempting a comeback. We were with him at a French social event, and he invited us to the Bastille Parade to take place at the French headquarters the next day. I assumed that he had reservations for us in the reviewing stand.

###

The next morning, we were having coffee in the Commander's Office. The Company Commander was on leave so the Executive Officer was in charge. We were discussing if we should skip duty and go to the parade.

The Executive Officer said, "let's go."

"Why not, let's do go."

###

We didn't have time to obtain approval from higher headquarters, but we thought it would be okay since we were doing our best to enhance French and American relationships.

###

We got into my car, and we were on our way to further international contacts. We were the last car to arrive and were directed down a small road to the parking area. The road passed between the reviewing stand on the right and the French military, in formation, on the left. We were just in time and had 10 minutes to park and take our seats. We walked up to the stands to be seated. At the entrance was an impressive French Officer greeting everyone and then having them escorted to their seats.

The French Officer had a puzzled look on his face while looking at the rank of two First Lieutenants.

He checked the list and, with a smirk on his face said, "You don't seem to be on the list."

While he had been looking at his reservations, I took a closer look at the occupants in the stand. It turned out to be a VIP reviewing stand. They were all Generals and Colonels of the French, British, Russian, and United States military. It was obvious we were in the wrong place. We immediately started to leave. The French Officer saw the embarrassed look on my face and, at the same time, had a mischievous look on his face.

He told us, "Wait, there are two seats available. Two Russian generals failed to show, and I'll put you both into their seats."

These seats were right in the center on the second row. As we were being seated, I noticed my Battle Group commander (Colonel) and the U.S. Commander, Berlin (General)seated in lesser seats of prestige, several rows behind us. Now, we were certain we were not supposed to be there. No one said anything. If the General had noticed, he may have reflected on his days as a Lieutenant or maybe he couldn't believe he was being upstaged.

###

It was August 1959, time to take leave (vacation) for two weeks and travel throughout Europe. I had become friends with our Engineer Platoon Leader who was a Civil Engineer and had been on his college swimming team. He was interested in a European tour, so we put together our itinerary. Gas was eleven cents per gallon when purchased on a military installation, I loaded the trunk of the Buick with five-gallon cans of gas.

We toured Austria, Switzerland, the French Riviera, Monte Carlo, Pisa, Milan, Rome, Naples, Pompeii, and numerous other designations. When we arrived at a town, we went to the American Express Office for both a place to stay and then, we signed up for four-dollar tours. In 1959, we could walk in without prior reservations.

###

Our small tour group of the Vatican was exceptional. We even visited the 28 steps (Scala Sancta) at the nearby Lateran Palace. These were the steps that contained Christ's blood as he was judged by Pontius Pilate before he was crucified. The steps were brought from Jerusalem by Saint Helena in the fourth century. The steps were covered by wood to protect them, however, since 2019 the marble has been exposed and worshippers are allowed to ascend the steps on their knees. It was not crowded even though this was the summer tourist season. Europe was not overrun with sightseers in 1959.

CHAPTER 20.

Back in Berlin, I was at a social event when an attractive girl sought me out. That's always great for your ego, and we started dating, who wouldn't? I don't remember what she said her job was, as I had mentioned, Berlin was a hotbed of international intrigue. Little did I realize; I was about to be recruited to be a Soviet spy. I had no idea what was taking place; however, unusual circumstances began to happen.

She asked me, "Could you get a copy of your officer's duty roster. My dad sells insurance, he thinks that officers would be good clients."

This seemed to be inappropriate even though the roster is unclassified.

"I'll see what I can do."

Later, she brought her dad to my apartment for an introduction. It was strange that he would come to my apartment, why hadn't I been invited to their apartment or house? He didn't look old enough to be her dad.

His visit was more like an interrogation. "What unit are you in? How long will you be in Berlin? What are your responsibilities in your unit, are you making the Army a career?"

He was trying to appear to be friendly, but these seemed to be strange questions for a dad. For some reason, I answered in generalities.

After an hour they left. I noted he hadn't talked about insurance.

###

A week later she invited me to a party at her family apartment, and I agreed. I was greeted by her and her dad, but no mother. As I looked around, the place was lit by candles placed on low tables. I could barely see the shadows of 10 women and 20 men. The apartment took up the entire second floor. Most Germans had a simple apartment, not an entire level. It was difficult to see faces in the dim candlelight. As the guest of honor, I was seated in a chair surrounded by candles. My eyes had not adjusted, everyone could see me, but I couldn't see the other guests who were standing with faces far above the candles on the tables. After a while I stood up to socialize, but I still couldn't see faces clearly. Finally, the party was over, and I left.

###

My new, mysterious date, continued to press me for the duty roster. It didn't seem appropriate to give it to people outside the organization. I guess their plan was once I provided one document, it would be easier to encourage me to get others. As a First Lieutenant, I had little access to classified material, however, they believed once I got into the habit of passing unclassified information and we became friends, perhaps they thought it would be hard for me to refuse passing other information. They could put me into their files and when I was a higher rank, and I had access to Top Secret papers, they would renew old friendships. If that didn't work, they would resort to other measures to force cooperation. I didn't provide the roster and terminated the uncomfortable relationship with this odd girl.

###

Not long after our last date, I was told by the Company Commander that I had been selected to attend a class being given by our counter-intelligence unit. I was delighted that I was the only one selected to attend the class to represent our company. It sounded like fun. When I arrived for the instruction, there were only five other students. There were more instructors than students.

The opening remark by the instructor was, "With the proper incentives, one or two percent of personnel can be turned by foreign governments into being a spy with the proper incentives."

That was a high percentage, I can't believe that many people would sell out. In a Regiment of 3,000 men, 30 to 60 soldiers could become potential spies.

The instructor went on to explain, "Spies are recruited by the Soviets by offering money or through blackmail, which were frequently successful tools. Then counter-intelligence instructor arrived at the part that was more distressing for me.

"An alluring girl might be used to encourage espionage." He illustrated examples.

That seems like my recent experience. Is that possible? I still can't believe I would be a target. They keep emphasizing that one or two percent will turn.

This was too close to my experience to be happenstance.

The class ended, and I started to go back to my company when the instructor called me back, "Lieutenant Damrill, he pulled out a picture from a black folder, do you know the girl in this picture?"

I was surprised to see the girl I had been dating was in the photograph.

"Yes, I used to date her, but she seemed more interested in my duty roster for her dad who sells insurance, than in me. I'm not seeing her anymore."

"That's good that you won't be seeing her. It's possible that counterintelligence might call you in again."

###

A few days later, it dawned on me that it was not coincidence that I was the only one chosen from my company to attend the class since it occurred after I started dating this mysterious girl.

Was this a sting operation, was it a deliberate effort to entrap me? Had I been seen unknowingly associating with spies, and followed by people in counterintelligence?

This was the only formal counterintelligence briefing I received my entire career. No more was said, and things continued as normal. Glad I didn't pass the Duty Roster.

###

In December 1959, the Executive Officer and I took a trip to Copenhagen, Denmark. We had planned to go all the way to Stockholm, Sweden. The snow slowed us down stopping us at Copenhagen, Denmark, a country of four million five hundred thousand. Of course, we toured the nightclubs.

At one of the clubs, I remember saying, to our waiter, "There's a good-looking girl."

Our waiter responded with a chuckle, "Check again."

Oh, this is a floor show where the person doesn't turn out to be as expected. It is a female impersonator!

That evening they also had a burlesque show. It was one of the classiest presentations I have ever seen. The performer flirted with nudity; she was always behind a sheer curtain. Fantastic!

In fact, this club was the top-rated entertainment facility in that area. Sometime that evening, we were introduced to a Denmark Prince, or so they said. He was in the record business. They commented everyone is going to continue the party after the club closed and we were invited. However, it seemed out of place since some of the men seemed feminine.

###

Denmark had a constitutional monarchy (no real power). I found out later he was Prince Gorm (1919 – 1991), who lost his line of succession due to a 1953 succession law that stated an individual must be a direct descendant of King Christian X. Unfortunately, he was a nephew. One thing he didn't lose was any of his names. His full name was Prinz Goren Christian Frederik Hans Harald til Denmark.

###

One officer in our company was a pilot. To keep his rating current, he had to fly 4 hours a month. One day he landed his helicopter in our company area and asked, "How about keeping me company while I fly over Berlin?"

"That's a great idea!"

I jumped into the co-pilot seat and positioned my headset. We lifted off and flew low over the entire American Sector. It was a windy day, we could feel the force of the wind pushing the helicopter around. From our altitude, we could see most of the bombed-out buildings in East Berlin. The city had one of those high towers with a restaurant on top. We flew close to the windows waving at diners. While watching the patrons, the pilot became distracted. In our enthusiasm, we got too close to the tower. Then a gust of wind blew us even closer and got our adrenaline flowing.

Just missing a collision with the tower, the pilot commented in a nervous voice, "That was a tight maneuver".

I yelled back, "Should we try again? We need a better look at their expressions."

###

In January 1960, I received orders for my new assignment in the United States. I was to depart Germany on March 1960 and proceed to Fort Benning, Georgia for a ten-week Motor Officer Course. A Motor Officer was one of many of the additional duties of an Infantry Officer in a combat unit. This was an opportunity to learn the details of vehicle maintenance. After the school, I was scheduled to proceed to Fort Lewis, Washington for assignment to the 4th Infantry Division.

###

You could select transportation by ship or air on the return trip to the United States. I chose to return by ship. This would be a ten-day vacation on the open sea, transiting the Atlantic Ocean. A few military personnel were selected to travel on the SS United States ocean liner (America's flagship), this ship still holds the record for the fastest crossing of the Atlantic by an ocean liner between New York and Liverpool, England. It took three days, ten hours, and forty minutes. It had a top speed of 36 knots or 44 miles per hour. This record was set in 1952. In its day, it sailed with the likes of Prince Rainier, Marlin Brando, and Elizabeth Taylor, however to me the most fascinating was German spy Franz Joseph Stigler and Erwin Wilhelm Siegler who were crew members in 1941. These two spies were part of a group of 31 who were caught as part of the largest FBI-convicted spy group, the Duquesne Spy Ring.

However, I was selected to travel on the last remaining troop ship from WW II, the 'Darby'. The Darby had many jobs throughout her career, an escort, a school ship (training), convoy, and patrol. She was out of commission in 1947 but called back to duty in 1950. She was called on to ship troops from Germany to New York. That's when I boarded her in March 1960 at Bremerhaven, Germany. This ship took 10 days including one stop in Southampton, England. Many years later, the Darby finally ended up in the bottom of the sea as a sunken practice target off an island in Puerto Rico.

###

In the 1960's, the United States had a strong dollar internationally. This made It possible to purchase a German-made car, in Germany, far below the purchase price in the United States. The military allowed active-duty soldiers to ship one car to the United States freight-free. To ship a second car the serviceman would have to pay the shipping cost. Even after paying for the freight on the second car, it was possible to make a profit. To exploit this difference, I decided to purchase a Volkswagen (VW) Beatle for my use and purchase the least expensive Porsche Convertible, to be sold at a profit. The cost of the VW Bug was twelve hundred dollars, and the Porsche convertible was eighteen hundred dollars.

I shipped the Porsche to New York and the VW Bug to Washington State. I picked up the Porsche in New York and drove it for six months from New York to Fort Benning, Georgia, and then to Washington state. I sold the Porsche in Tacoma, Washington for a $700 profit. That was equivalent to two months' pay.

CHAPTER 21.1

I departed D.C. in the early morning and drove straight through, 750 miles to Fort Benning, Georgia. While driving, I thought this was an excellent opportunity to again volunteer to attend the Airborne and Ranger Schools upon completion of the Motor Officer Course. In 1957, I failed the required entry Physical Training Tests and was dropped from the classes for not being in top physical condition.

###

After 16 hours, I arrived at midnight and checked into Transit Bachelor Officer Quarters (BOQ). The next morning, I was assigned permanent quarters and a class schedule. While processing in, I also requested to attend the Airborne and Ranger Classes after I completed the Motor Officer Course. If I was accepted in the additional training, this would delay my reporting to Fort Lewis, WA, and would also require a change in orders for a new reporting date.

###

I was billeted in the same austere quarters, as I had while attending the Basic Officers Course in 1957. Student life is easy, but you are now one of numerous students at Fort Benning. There was none of the international intrigue that had preceded my lie's earlier adventures. Putting that disappointment aside, If I was accepted to attend the Airborne and Ranger schools, I had 10 weeks to get in shape while attending the Motor Officer course. My personal physical training program was simple. In my room was a small water pipe 18 inches from the ceiling and firmly attached. I would practice Airborne pull-ups on the pipes every time I entered the room. The Airborne school required six pull-ups and was considered the required strength to guide a parachute. In preparation for Ranger School, I also practiced the Physical Training Test three times a week after my Mortor Officer classes. Two days a week I would go for a two-mile run. In ten weeks, I was able to get in shape and lost 20 pounds in the process.

###

Class started with 40 to 50 officers in attendance. Class instruction was low-key. I was surprised to see how simple vehicles were when disassembled. Since the class was at the Infantry School, we focused only on light vehicles such as jeeps three-quarter ton, and two and one-half ton trucks. In addition to learning vehicle repair, we learned how to set up and operate a maintenance shop, how to order repair parts, and how much to keep in stock. We set up maintenance schedules, kept records, and ensured safety practices. We had the weekends free, and it was appreciated because troop units worked Saturday mornings.

###

On my first weekend, I started exploring Georgia recreation areas near Fort Benning. I quickly found a great location called Callaway Gardens. It was a terrific recreational area one hour from Fort Benning. It was a terrific place to unwind and relax. It had a small sandy beach on a large lake with a concession stand which was surrounded by lush gardens. I bought a beach towel and rented an umbrella for shade to lounge under the pleasant Georgia sky. Life was good with few worries. It was like being on vacation in the Caribbean.

While hanging out, I ran into a couple of married First Lieutenants who had been in my college ROTC class. One Lieutenant was also from my high school graduation class. They were on temporary duty at Fort Benning for a few days attending conferences. That same weekend, and before meeting the Lieutenants, I met a girl who could have been a model for swimsuits. She was from a small nearby college. When the girl and I later met the Lieutenants, I could see that they were impressed by the envy expressed in their eyes. We all had a wonderful afternoon. The girl and I met a few more times at the beach and had a couple of other dates. Then the school year ended, and she was gone. This is often the story of relationships because of my transitory status.

###

The college this girl attended had been an all-girl college, but now it was co-ed and had about 20 guys enrolled. My timing for attending college was off. If I were a few years younger I could have enrolled in college as the male student number 21. A lucky 21!

###

Nearby the Callaway Gardens was President Franklin Delano Roosevelt's Little White House in Warm Springs, Georgia. He first came to Warm Springs in 1924 hoping to find a cure for infantile Paralysis. (polio) that had struck him in 1921. Swimming in the 88-degree, buoyant spring waters did not bring him the healing he sought, but it did bring some comfort. The Little White House was built in 1932 while he was Governor of New York. The house had a lovely forest environment close to the Springs. The home was tiny by modern standards. FDR was visited there by Lucy Rutherford, a decades-old and intimate friend who was present when he suffered his fatal stroke. Elinore had learned of this affair many years earlier; nevertheless, she remained FDR's closest adviser and friend.

FDR struggled with the Great Depression with various New Deal efforts to aid the economy with only mild successes; however, he did initiate the Social Security Act of 1935, unemployment insurance, and aid for dependent children and the disabled.

###

While attending the Motor Officer Course in 1960, President Eisenhower visited Fort Benning. All students on post lined up along the route of the President motorcade. As he passed along the route he rode sitting on top of the back seat of a convertible waving to the crowd. The event had the enthusiasm and feel of a 4th of July parade. This five-star General became the US's 34th president after his role as the Supreme Commander of the Allied Expeditionary Force in Europe in WW II and the director of the Normandy Invasion D Day, 6 June 1944. He promoted the 1957 Civil Rights Act integrating schools and connected America with the Interstate Highway System. Most of all, we honored him as one of us, amid-west West Point General and hero of all Americans.

###

After the celebration of Eisenhower's visit, we returned to class to the safety portion of our instruction which stressed the training of drivers. The instructors referred to the accident I was in in 1957 where the truck had rolled over killing two students and in jurying 20 others. The young driver was driving the last truck at an excessive speed trying to catch up with the convoy. He was speeding and going downhill on a gravel road and attempted a sharp turn at the bottom. The truck rolled. The cause of this accident was attributed to the driver in the lead vehicle driving too fast for the other vehicles in the convoy to maintain the proper distances. The high speed of the lead vehicle and the varying traffic speeds cause an accordion effect, with the last vehicle always trying to catch up.

###

It was May of 1960 and the closing week of the Motor Officer Course. During the proceeding period, the students were given several written and pragmatic tests. For example, the student was presented with a disabled vehicle and required to diagnose the problem. Fix it and upon completion drive the vehicle to its parking place. We were given grades, but they were not posted. At most Infantry Schools the scores were posted, without names, so you could determine your standing.

A couple of days before the final test, the lead instructor commented on how close the competition was for the top spot. Five students were tied for the number one position.

Who could that be? No one knows their standings. Anyway, I'm sure I'm not in that group.

One of the senior non-commissioned NCO's instructors, who had access to test scores, that I had become friends with, saw the look of puzzlement on my face and came over to talk.

"Lieutenant Damrill, you know you're one of the top five"

"That's a surprise. The final test is tomorrow. That will be interesting. Who are the other competitors?"

"Sorry, I'm not allowed to say."

###

The final test was to be administered the next day. Not much time to prepare. After the test, no final grade was provided, and no other comments concerning class standings. A couple of days later at graduation the top three were given special recognition. After the ceremony was over, the NCO instructor, I had previously talked with before the final test came over to talk. He was really upset about something.

"Lieutenant Damrill you were third, but they changed the scores so you would be fourth. They wanted to give the third spot to a student officer who was assigned to be an instructor and leader in the academic branch that taught vehicle maintenance courses."

What could I say? The NCO believed in fair play and just saw all the rules violated. He is disappointed in their rigging of the system. I guess they felt that a future instructor needed to have bragging rights.

That's a tough break. Thanks, that's nice to know and great for the ego that I was really third. I guess the goal was to make their future boss happy. Thanks again, hope to see you again. I'm going to try my luck as a student over at the Airborne School."

###

After graduation, I proceeded to the Airborne School and reported for duty. The next morning, we assembled in a class formation of about 100 students. First on the agenda was the Physical Training Test. This time I was in good condition and easily passed. We ran everywhere. Well, it was sort of a run. We would do a shuffle run for four minutes and walk for two minutes.

###

The first phase of training was to practice parachute landing falls (PLF's). When descending in a parachute you oscillate and can land forward, sidewise, or to the rear. To train for these landings, we practiced jumping from a four-foot platform with our bodies facing to the front, left side, right side, an rear. Upon landing, our knees are bent, and you roll, or tumble in the direction of the simulated oscillation. The purpose of this drill was to develop an automatic response when hitting the ground to minimize injury. When your feet touch the ground, you can't think fast enough to tumble in the right direction. It must be a developed instinct. Intermingled with this physical training were classes on how weather, such as air density and wind can affect the jumper.

In this phase, you were also taught what to do if landing in a high wind and how to quickly release your chute to prevent being dragged over the ground. For the practical exercise, you were placed on the ground, in a prone position, in a harness with the attached parachute. The school had a large wind machine that filled the parachute and dragged you across the ground. The student had only seconds to release the chute to receive a satisfactory grade. The reason for this training? In combat, you may be required to jump during adverse weather conditions.

###

Phase two was jumping from a 34-foot tower. On top of the tower was a mockup of an aircraft door. You were taught the proper body position when exiting the aircraft and the correct body position while descending. After the student demonstrated proper proficiency in these tasks he proceeded to the tower.

###

On top of the tower, the student stood in the door, and on the instructor's command, you jumped from the door. You were attached to two 10-foot cables that were connected to a pully on a zip line. At the end of the 10-foot fall, you received a powerful jerk and then glided down the zip line with an instructor grading your performance during the exit and the slide down the zip line, which simulates descending in a parachute.

###

Phase three was being dropped by parachute from a 250-foot tower. With a parachute overhead, you were hoisted up 250 feet, and on the command of the instructor below, released for a free fall and drifted to the ground below. Part of this training was to instruct you on how to guide your parachute in an attempt to avoid obstacles, and If it was a windy day, how to guide your parachute into the wind to reduce drift speed. In addition, you were taught how to deploy your reserve parachute in case of malfunction of the main chute. In 1960 parachutes were only slightly steerable. Once released the instructors gave tutoring, over a handheld megaphone, on which way to guide your parachute to avoid hitting the tower as well as remaining in the circular drop zone area surrounding the tower.

On my first drop there was marginal weather, thin atmospheric air, and a slight breeze. The chute descended rapidly, and I hit hard. As luck would have it, I slightly twisted my right knee. I carefully stood up, so the instructor wouldn't notice the injury. I didn't want to be dropped from the class. Fortunately, I could run straight, if I didn't try side movements.

On the next drop, I tried landing on my left leg to protect the injured right knee. This was not a good idea because you could break that leg. The instructor noticed my incorrect landing, and I received a severe reprimand. However, he gave the okay for me to proceed to phase four which was exiting an aircraft in flight.

###

In phase four, we loaded our aircraft for our first jump. The aircraft flew a short pattern to the drop zone, enabling enough time to attain the jump altitude of 1,000 feet and go through the procedures of standing up, hooking up your static line, and checking your equipment. You were so busy you didn't have time to be scared. The green light goes on and everyone starts shuffling toward the door. You must exit quickly while the aircraft is over the drop zone. If you come out too late you can end up in the trees. Everyone is pushing toward the door and all of a sudden, you're out. You can feel the parachute opening and then you're gliding to the ground. Fortunately, I was able to favor my bad knee without another injury. We completed four more jumps and received our Parachute Wings on the drop zone after the fifth jump. Seventy-five percent passed the course, and one in four failed.

###

With the injured knee, I knew I would have to postpone attending Ranger School. After a change in orders, I proceeded to Fort Lewis, Washington with a short stop in Pittsburg, Kansas. I was 27.

CHAPTER 21.2

-

I arrived in Bremerhaven, Germany in March 1960 and boarded the troop ship "Darby." The troops went below and were berthed four or five high, similar to what I experienced in the USMC when aboard a Navy ship in 1952. Junior Officers were billeted four to a cabin. I'm not sure what the arrangements were for families or Senior Officers. There was a high level of excitement while everyone boarded and then the ship departed port in the morning.

After a brief voyage across the English Channel, we docked in Southampton, England in the afternoon for an overnight stay. We took on additional freight and passengers and were given liberty until 9 A.M. the next day.

One of the officers in our cabin said, "Let us four go to London."

The other three responded simultaneously, "Yes." We boarded a train for London and arrived at about 6 P.M. and proceeded to Trafalgar Square looking for excitement and sightseeing. After we had been there about two hours, looking like a typical lost tourist, we were approached by a Brit about 30 years old.

"You chaps looking for a good time with a lot of excitement."

"Sure, where can we go?

"I know just the place. Follow me."

We thought it would be a place just around the corner on one of the main streets. That didn't happen. We followed him several blocks down side streets.

Where is he taking us? Should we ditch him and head back to the square?

"Here it is on the second floor. We must go up the fire escape."

What, I thought was we were going to a club! Now, we're in for it. Oh well, this is really something different.

We climbed the fire escape and entered through a large window. Greeting us were five or six girls in the room. In the corner was a small bar. I noticed the entire floor was a series of mattresses placed together and covered the entire floor space.

WOW!! That did it, red flags started flying, and this place looked like trouble. If we were given knockout drops in our drinks or mugged, we would never make it back to the ship. There are no excuses acceptable for missing a troop movement.

We all had the same idea and quickly withdrew back through the window, down the fire escape, and back to the square.

That was close. I guess we are not real-world travelers yet.

We hung out on the square for a couple more hours and then headed back to Southampton to reboard our ship.

###

At 9 A.M. we departed port and headed for New York City. The deck resembled a cruise ship. However, no was entertainment, so I read a book to pass the time in the cabin. Outside on the deck, it was cold, and the sea was rough, and I noticed I was getting a slight case of seasickness.

I met a girl traveling with her parents who lived in Seattle, Washington. We planned to meet for a date in Seattle in the fall. Unfortunately, I got only the address and not the phone number.

###

About eight days later we arrived in New York harbor and passed the Statue of Liberty before docking. It was quite an event when we docked. A band played, ticker tape filled the air, and some passengers had family and friends waiting to greet them. It was impressive.

Is this what it's like when soldiers returned from World War II?

###

After debarking the ship, I proceeded to a nearby dock area where my Porsche had been shipped and was waiting for my pickup. As I mentioned earlier, there was a Lieutenant I knew in Berlin whose dad wanted him to leave the Army and join him on Wall Street. He agreed and when he left Berlin in 1959, he invited me to visit. After I picked up my car, I gave him a call. He wanted me to see his office. Even though he had been there less than a year, he had his own office which was quite extraordinary.

After a short meeting, he asked, "How about you stay overnight at my house on Long Island and meet my wife."

"Looks like it will be a great evening."

###

That evening, I followed him through the traffic. I had never seen so many cars, with headlights on, bumper-to-bumper for miles departing New York City for Long Island.

When we arrived, the house was spectacular. A year before, he had been living in a one-bedroom apartment and now lived in a gated community in a very upscale house. His wife was definitely part of the social society and very attractive. Fortunately, I drove up in a Porsche, a car that would be acceptable to the neighbors while parked in the driveway. It was a pleasant evening, and I departed the next morning to Washington, D.C. I should have kept track of him but failed to do so. Being from Kansas I didn't realize the value of networking.

###

Arriving in Washington, D.C. I remembered that the Engineer Platoon Leader Lieutenant with whom I had toured southern Europe, had asked me to drop by for a visit when I arrived in D.C. He had left Berlin a few months earlier and secured a lucrative Engineering position in D.C. I gave him a call and he took me on a tour of all the best nightclubs in the area. There were plenty of aspiring, ambitious single 20- and 30-year-old men and women in D.C. It was a terrific night.

###

Completing social engagements, I decided to go by the Pentagon to check my efficiency reports (report card). In the 1950's you didn't see your written report and were told verbally, in general terms, by your first rater, about job performance. The second rater or endorser never provided input. The first rater is your immediate commander, and the second rater is your commander's boss or someone on his staff. The rater and endorser each count for 50 percent. Based on what I had been told verbally by the raters (my commanders) I thought I had done well for a Second Lieutenant and a new First Lieutenant.

In the 50's and 60's officers had to go to the Pentagon to review your reports, which was very inconvenient. The officers assigned to critique you were generally on a fast track and were later promoted to General. It appeared they were given this assignment for a short time. I guess this assignment allowed them to overview the caliber of Officers in the Army.

There was a secondary purpose for my visit. I was told the receptionist was an unbelievably good-looking single girl, better than Marilyn Monroe. I was sure I could get a date. That didn't happen. Unfortunately, I had been misinformed and the receptionist was a charming middle-aged married woman. There must have been a personnel change, or had I been talking to older officers who had visited the Pentagon when they were younger?

When you check in with the receptionist, she retrieves your file, and you are allowed to read your efficiency reports before you visit with the interviewing officer. The reports were okay, but not impressive. I was disappointed. My critique officer came out with a warm welcome and invited me into his office. We exchanged a few words and then got down to business.

"How did I do? How did I rate?"

"Well, you are in the one percent bracket."

WOW, I can be a General. Wait, that's too high and doesn't sound right. My reports weren't that impressive.

"That's the top one percent?"

He smiled slightly, "No, that's the bottom one percent"

I was stunned. From what I read in my reports, before going in, and based on my rater's verbal report, I was above average. How can anyone score that low? First a general and now the last man in line.

"That's really low, should I resign?"

Why was he smiling like he was enjoying this interview? Was there more information in my file that I didn't know about?

"You were a single Second Lieutenant in Berlin and are still in uniform. You will be okay, and you should stay in the Army."

Had other single officers assigned to Berlin received similar ratings?

He vaguely explained that efficiency reports have a relatively flat curve and a few points can make a huge difference in your standing.

This reminded me of my days in the USMC and evaluations. In the USMC we were rated 1 to 9. The officer rating members in my company thought you had to be standing next to God to get a 9. The adjacent company rating officer thought that most should get a 9. The scores went to USMC Headquarters to determine who should be promoted to corporal. Some of us received an 8 in our company, but only those who had received a 9 were promoted. Our company got zero promotions, and the adjacent company received the promotions. Again, this is an example of a flat curve. We concluded the interview, and I departed the office with a bruised ego. I went to the parking lot hopped into my Porsche, put the top down, and headed for a new adventure waiting for me at Fort Benning. The sun was out, the wind was blowing in my face as I sped down the highway in my sports car.

CHAPTER 22.

Before leaving Georgia, I thought of the model I had known in Berlin, Germany. She had given me her sister's address in northern Georgia. I decided to visit to find out how her sister was doing in the modeling business. I gave her a call and she was excited to have a visitor from her hometown of Berlin. I located her address in the early afternoon and received a warm welcome. She was quite attractive. We sat on the large porch of the upper middle-income house, drinking Mint Juleps. After two or three hours, it was time to depart. I commented,

"It's been a great afternoon."

"Thanks for stopping by. Oh, my sister wanted me to give you her current address."

"Thanks, hope to see you again."

It had been a great afternoon with overwhelming hospitality.

###

On the road to Pittsburg, I recalled I had become part owner of a cab company in Fort Scott, Kansas, a town 30 miles North of Pittsburg. I decided to drop by for an unannounced visit prior to my my trip to my hometown.

###

Excited to see the business, I pulled in front of the dispatch office in my new sports car. The dispatch office is where the company receives calls from customers and the dispatcher gives the request to one of the drivers. In 1960 there were no cell phones, so all calls came through the company office. We did have radios.

I had high expectations that they would be interested in me the partner who had been in Europe. When I entered the door, I was engulfed in cigarette smoke with cigarette butts all over the floor. The place was a shambles, the drivers were poorly dressed, and I noticed the parked taxis out the window were in bad repair. I introduced myself.

"Hi, I'm Ron Damrill, one of the part owners whose name is on the front door. I've been in Berlin for the past few years while serving in the Army. I thought I would drop by for a visit and introduce myself."

To my surprise, they were less than interested, especially when they looked out the door and saw my sports car parked in their space. It became obvious that they were unconcerned who the partners were and had received few visits from management. They thought were running the company. I left after a few minutes, dismayed at what I encountered, but I was glad I stopped.

###

Arriving home, I was greeted by my youngest sister, Faye, (age 15), and my mom. My mother had just graduated from college with a teaching degree at age 50. She had acquired a teaching position at Fort Leavenworth, Kansas, a town 110 miles north and slightly west of Pittsburgh. My 24-year-old married sister lived close by, in Kansas City. My mother's position was desirable because the salary on base was significantly higher than other positions in Kansas. Another bonus was her working conditions. There were few discipline problems in her school. If a child acted up, his military father was quickly summoned to the base commander's office for guidance concerning his student's behavior in the classroom. In short, if the soldier wanted to have a successful career, he had better put his house in order.

###

After a brief visit, we went over to my grandparents' house for dinner. My step-grandad, Art was an artillery combat veteran of World

War One (WW I) and had fought many artillery duels with the Germans in 1917 and 1918.

"Hi, grandad."

"Let's hear all about your military adventures!"

He was anxious to reminisce.

My grandmother Allie chimed in.

"How about me, come over and give me a hug."

As soon as dinner was over, my more charming than ever, younger sister was getting ready to depart on a date. The local boys noticed her developing good looks. A boy named Rick showed up at the door to pick her up and brief introductions were made.

"We want her back, you know." I directed toward the young man who would eventually become her future husband.

"Oh, you didn't have to say that." My sister exclaimed as she embarrassingly directed this red-faced boy out the door.

###

The next day I decided to visit the Taxi and Bus Company of Pittsburg, Kansas. Before going to the company, I stopped for a visit at the college Student Union where I met several friends who had gone into education and were attending summer school, as they worked on their master's degree. While visiting, an exceptionally good-looking girl student from Hawaii joined the group. After an hour, most of the group departed for classes except for the Hawaiian girl and me. We talked for a few minutes before she agreed to go on a date later in the day.

###

Before departing, I went up to the concession stand for a cup of coffee. There I met a congenial woman I knew who had been working in the concession stand for years. She was delighted to see a previous student. Then her demeanor changed.

"You own the bus company?"

"Yes, I'm part owner."

"Your buses never run on time. What can you do about it?"

Stunned I responded, "I'm going over to the company now and will see what is going on."

###

No longer enthused about my visit to the company, I trudged over to see what was occurring. I didn't have any illusions of changing anything since I would only be in Pittsburgh for a few days.

###

Word had already gotten around I was in town, and they were expecting my visit. I was well received, and I knew several of the employees. After a short visit, one well-dressed employee I had previously known, asked if I would have a cup of coffee with him. He was a sharp guy and had been a senior NCO (E-7) in World War Two (WW II). We agreed to meet at the local coffee shop in 30 minutes.

###

At the coffee shop, we sat down at a corner table. I could tell he had something on his mind but wasn't sure he should confide in me. Finally, his frustration was more than he could handle, and he started talking.

"The business was being run by your partner's parents. Furthermore, they didn't want the responsibility of management."

He went on to say.

"No one is actively managing the company, and your partner is draining the company dry of dollars to pay for his college Law Degree. There are no funds left to improve equipment or to better working conditions for employees. Everything is in disarray. His parents don't want to run the company. His mom is reluctantly collecting the money and paying a few bills. His dad is doing minimal maintenance on the vehicles."

Damn it, my partner is taking all the profit and selling off some of the assets??

"I'm here for a few days, what can I do for long-term effect?"

"You can make me a manager and I will get the company running properly. The other employees support the idea."

How can I do this in two weeks?

"That's a lot of information, let me think this over and see what I can work out."

We continued our conversation for another hour talking about the company and how the city was changing, and other business activities were advancing.

###

Another hour later I was headed back to the company's office as I was thinking about my previous conversation.

My partner is cheating the company, taking all the profit and selling off some of the assets from the company for Law School., and not working. I didn't expect to receive any financial return, since I wasn't working either. A transit company in Pittsburg doesn't make much money. All profits should go to those doing the work.

I felt the perspiration from my disappointment accumulating on my face and neck, moistening my shirt.

###

An hour later I returned to the headquarters and my partner's mom was there doing some paperwork. The person I had just talked to was sitting within listening distance. The mom and I exchanged pleasantries, and I received an update on how my partner was doing in law school. After a period, I said.

"Just to pass the time. may I look at the books and see how things are going?"

The mom immediately displayed a hostile look and slowly started closing the drawers to the desk.

"The books are at home, and I'll bring them by tomorrow."

Tension filled the air in her office and in the adjacent dispatch room, where drivers were waiting for a customer call. They were in hearing distance of the conversation.

What a day!!

###

I left all the negativity and prepared for my date with the good-looking Hawaiian girl. I picked her up at the dorm and I could see she was impressed with my Porsche sports car. It was a warm summer evening, and we drove with the top down. There weren't a lot of places to go on a date in Pittsburgh, but we were having a great time. Then towards the end of the date, she suddenly realized.

"I guess you are just here briefly, you'll soon be going back to your Army assignment. I am anxious to go back to Hawaii and want to have a stationary life there. I guess that limits our future dating."

"That would make it challenging,." I regrettably responded. That ended our relationship. Interestingly, in the fall semester, she was elected Homecoming Queen.

###

The next day I dropped by the office, at the agreed time, to review the books.

"Hi, do you have the books," with a forced smile on my face.

"I can't seem to get them organized. My son said he would like you to drop by for dinner in Topeka, while on your way to Fort Lewis, Washington. He will go over everything at that time."

It's obvious she isn't going to cooperate or provide any information and doesn't even want to talk to me. I can't blame her She and her husband had been the ones stuck with all the effort; but from my view, it looks like a previous friend has become dishonest. I hope I'm wrong.

I knew when I left for the Army that I would have little say in the business. I had enjoyed setting up the company while in college and had hoped this would provide a point of contact with my hometown. I had borrowed only $1,500 to invest for my share of the company. My loan had been paid off and I wasn't financially concerned about my small investment, even though $1,500 represented a one-half-year salary, for local employees in Pittsburg. I was disappointed with the poor customer service and its reflection on my reputation. On the positive side, owning a small part of a company made a great conversation subject at social events.

CHAPTER 23.

After leaving the taxicab office, I dropped by the main drug store in town about two blocks from the office, for a sandwich. In the 1960's most drug stores had a lunch counter. Sitting next to me was a student nurse at our local hospital. We struck up a conversation and she agreed to go to lunch the next day.

###

For the lunch date, I thought it would be impressive showing up in my officer's uniform and driving a sports car. I picked her up at the hospital and we headed to a local restaurant. Things were going smoothly; however, halfway through the meal she asked,

"What are you wearing?"

Somewhat surprised, "It's an Army Officer Uniform."

She has no idea what I was talking about. Waist of my effort.

She responded, "Oh."

After the uniform confusion, we had several dates going to the local swimming hole at the edge of town where many of the locals' young adults hung out and could launch a small ski boat. The swimming hole was one of many old coal strip mines that had filled with water and was as wide and as long as three football fields. This location was much better than the city swimming pool where all the young kids ruled the pool.

###

Pittsburg's early expansion had come mostly from coal mining. My ancestors, particularly both my grandad and step-granddad had settled in the area due to the employment opportunities in coal mining. My granddad from Sweden worked out of the Minden Mines, Missouri,

10 miles east of Pittsburg. My step-granddad worked out of the Pittsburg area.

###

The coalfields in Pittsburg and surrounding areas were the longest continuous operating mines in the United States, covering over 300 square miles. In the 1800's, coal was so close to the surface that it could be picked up and taken home to warm a house. By 1929, 150 shaft mines and strip mining sprung up in the Pittsburg and Minden Mines area. The underground mines were dangerous as my Swedish, grandad, on my mom's side discovered in 1927. He had volunteered for a job as an explosive expert in Minden Mines. There were dangers associated with the job, but the extra pay made it an attractive choice. In his job he set the charges and then lit the fuses. The downside, if the fuse failed to work and the charge didn't explode, the person who had set the charge, had to go back into the mine to defuse the dynamite. On two occasions the fuse did a slow burn and when he went to defuse the charge it exploded. The first time he was able to recover and be back on the job in a year. The second time the explosion blinded him for life.

Underground mining had miners working on their hands and knees since the shafts were not tall. In a mine explosion in 1885 one hundred and seventy-six miners were killed when gasses exploded.

My step-grandad, in the 1930s through to the 1950's, participated in strip mining. The coal is close to the surface, and it is dug up by a steam shovel. We called them steam shovels, but they were later converted to diesel. There were 43 shovels in operation and my step-granddad operated one. Over 9,000 men were working in the coal mining industry around the Pittsburg area. The strip-mining process would begin by identifying the coal fields and their depth; and finally, stripping the dirt from the ground down to the coal and removing it. Coal was then hauled away by teams of horses or mules. Later, with shaft and strip mining, coal was hauled away by railroad cars.

The shovels would go in straight lines and stack the dirt up on the side of the trench creating a large mound of dirt. After several hundred yards, the shovels would stop and start another row. The dirt stripped from this row would be dumped into the previously mined row. These created mounds of dirt 50 feet high. The last strip wouldn't be covered by dirt, leaving a large pit that eventually filled with water that could be more than 100 feet deep. These became swimming holes, places to water ski, and they also became filled with fish. Fishing became a popular sport though the fish were always uncomfortable nibbling on the swimmers. The mounds of dirt became overgrown and in the 1950's was a great place to hunt rabbits. There was no requirement for restoring the land, and these mounds of dirt are still present today.

###

Unfortunately, competition from the eastern coal mines diminished the importance of the Pittsburg area mines as the companies who had previously employed thousands moved to Denver, Colorado.

###

I was having a great time, but it was time to leave. I had noticed, during my visit, most of my friends had left town for better paying jobs. Having a company as a connection point for returning to Pittsburg to be with old friends, was a fantasy quickly fading. I was well-known during my high school and college years. I had appeared on the front page of the local newspaper several times and had other write-ups on the back pages. However, this was the past. Pittsburg was now the town I was from, not my home anymore. Its influence was diminishing.

###

Well, to my next adventure. Enroute, I would take time to visit my partner in Topeka. I still had faith in human integrity and was hoping my partner could explain the taxi situation. I expected him to say, that when he finished law school next year, he was going to return to Pittsburg to set up practice, run the business, and with his legal background explore other business opportunities in the city and surrounding area. I wanted to see his side of the story.

###

Arriving in Topeka, I drove up in front of their ground-floor apartment in my Porches sports car with the top down. I looked every bit like a rich single army Officer with money to burn. Little did they know I had just enough money in my pocket for gas and a sandwich for my trip to Fort Lewis. I timed my arrival to be just in time for cocktails and dinner with my partner and his family. The event was cordial, but there seemed to be a little tension in the air. He didn't seem like the same person I had known in High School and College. He seemed like one of those politicians that lie to you, realizing that you know that they are lying, and then asking for more money. Is he studying the wrong side of the law? During our drinking of adult refreshments and dinner, nothing was being said about the business and I assumed it would be discussed later.

Dinner was over and his wife put the kids to bed and returned. The conversation was going in circles, so I said.

"Your mom said you wanted to review the Balance Sheets and Profit and Loss Statements with me."

"They're not that important, I'll mail them to you at Fort Lewis."

I have a dishonest partner. Hell, as disorganized as they are, there may not be any readable books.

I went on to discuss my observations and a comment I had received from a customer.

"I dropped by the Fort Scott office, and it was in disarray. The woman we knew at the concession stand in the College Student Union said the busses didn't run on schedule."

He isn't interested.

"It appears your parents don't like the responsibility of running the company, and I have a solution. We have a sharp employee that was a Senior NCO (E7) in WW II who says he can make the company proficient and profitable. This would take the pressure off your parents."

He looks like I told him the Internal Revenue Service (IRS) was coming for an audit.

Irritated he responded,

"My parents are doing a good job and don't need outside help from an employee. The real problem is that we need an infusion of money to get everything back on track. Can you put $3,000 in the account?"

Christ, he wants money for his last year of law school. His wife is very nervous and in need of money. They are broke!

I was first irritated, then I was embarrassed to think he thought I was that gullible. Now it was my turn. Keeping up the image of a rich single Army Officer and feeling a little mischievous. I dragged the discussion on for a few minutes and finally said,

"Okay, let me see what I can do when I get to Fort Lewis. I'm sure I can arrange something."

He wants me to give him $3,000. That's a working man's annual wage. He has changed. Glad the evening is over.

As I departed, it was getting dark, and I drove for a while before stopping at a truck stop for a short nap in my front seat. Before I fell asleep, I reviewed my request for assignment. I had requested

Washington, D.C. I got Washington, but it was Washington State. My reasoning for applying to D.C. was that I heard there were four girls for every boy. Something was wrong with my career planning. I should have had a mentor to help me manage my career. One that would require me to stick to business, not recreation. I would advise acquiring a mentor early in anyone's career whether military or civilian.

Several of the Lieutenants I had served with in Berlin were also reassigned to Fort Lewis, Washington. We were lucky to be assigned to a troop combat unit, the 4th Infantry Division.

###

Having a Porsche sports car, I felt required to drive it like a race car. It was at 8:00 A.M. and I was approaching Denver, Colorado on a four-lane road. There was sparse traffic, and I was speeding along the freeway above the speed limit. I noticed a local police officer had stopped a car on the left side of the highway and headed in the opposite direction. It looked like he was giving the driver a ticket. I thought the police officer was busy and didn't have time for me. So, I didn't slow down. Within a few minutes, there were red flashing lights in my rearview mirror. I was pulled over. The officer came up and we started talking.

"I see from your Georgia license plate and military stickers on your windshield, that you're an officer from Fort Benning."

"that's correct, I have been reassigned to Fort Lewis, Washington."

"I was commissioned two years ago and had my Infantry training there."

A fellow officer won't give me a ticket.

"I'm sorry, I'll have to take you in to appear before a judge to receive your fine for speeding."

He escorted me to a judicial-style office to appear before a small-town judge for my speeding sentence. It was a short visit with the judge, as he quickly gave me a $150 fine. The fine was to be paid in cash immediately or go to jail. I had just enough money to buy gas to Washington. I was stuck in Colorado with only $40. I didn't know anyone I could ask to borrow $150, which was a half month's pay. Then I remembered, I was the half-owner of a Bus and Cab Company. I asked the judge.

"Can I have the money wired by Western Union?"

"That will be satisfactory, my patrol officer will escort you to the Western Union office."

"Can I use your phone to call for the money to be wired. I'll pay for the long-distance call."

I called the company in Pittsburg, and I was in luck when my partner's mom answered the phone. I explained the circumstances and asked if she could wire the $150. There were several seconds of silence. Finally, she reluctantly responded and agreed to send the money within the hour. It was a good choice, letting my partner believe that I would attempt to obtain an additional $3,000 for the business. I had a clear conscience since this was the only $150 replacement on my original $1,500 investment.

###

The patrol officer escorted me to the Western Union office. When the money arrived, he escorted me back before the judge and I paid the $150 which was equivalent to over $2,000 today. The Patrol Officer had spent half a day with me.

CHAPTER 24.

As soon as I crossed the Washington state line, everyone in a Porsche would honk their horn and wave. This must be Porsche country. Halfway across Washington, I drove over the Cascade Mountain Range. It was July 1960, and the sun was shining brightly, making the mountains appear majestic. I pulled off the road, found a level spot, took out my beach towel, and laid in the sun for a nap in the mountains.

###

I arrived at Fort Lewis a few days before my reporting date. This provided time to become familiar with the post, be assigned a bachelor's officer quarter (BOQ), get the proper patches sewn on my uniform, and accomplish other administrative tasks. I had extra time and sold my Porsche, which I had driven for six months for a 40 percent profit, and then picked up the Volkswagen Beetle (bug) I had shipped from Germany. After a couple of days, I decided to call my partner and tell him I didn't get the $3,000. It was a short conversation. He did manage to finish Law School and obtain an excellent position with a law firm in Topeka. Since neither of us were returning to Pittsburg, his parents refused to continue operating the company. My partner wanted to sell, and I agreed, provided there were no outstanding debts that I might be liable. He put it in writing and the business was sold. I was delighted to get out of a failing company without additional debt.

###

A few years later I met a mutual friend of myself and my ex-partner at a military conference. This friend had graduated with us from High School and College and went on active duty in the Army after graduation from college. He was the one person from our class, who knew all the scandals that befell members of the 1950 High School Class. At dinner, he couldn't wait to bring me up to date.

"Do you know what happened to your ex-partner?"

I was curious and responded, "No, what happened."

"He became involved in a scandal in Topeka. He was disbarred from law and his wife divorced him."

"Being disbarred isn't good. What happened after that."

"That's all I Know, "

"I'm disappointed, I remembered that he had the personality of an honest 1800's western sheriff. It looks like he tried to be a big-time politician, trying their dishonest ways. I'm guessing, his honesty resurfaced at the wrong time, and he was slammed with a trumped-up scandal, who knows?"

###

A few years later, I again ran into the same officer in Pittsburg. He was teaching Senior ROTC at the university. The college was previously named Kansas State Teachers College and now is Pittsburg State University. I asked him,

"Is there an update on my ex-partner?"

"Yes, he had to find a new career and returned to college and received a degree in agriculture. He obtained a job with a large agricultural company with a small office in Ford, Kansas".

Ford was a town of 200 residents just 18 miles southeast of Dodge City which had a population of 15,000 residents.

He continued, "Because of his popular position with the company, he was elected mayor." He wanted to be governor. Mayor got him part way."

"Say, I think you use to call him 'Thrifty Honest Abe' in high school? In retrospect, I think he started cutting money corners to finish Law School and then was hired by a crooked law firm. Looks like he has returned to his 'Thrifty Honest Abe' roots. He, has left the big city scandal behind and settled into a small town, becoming a political, civic, and business leader."

###

I finished settling into my BOQ. It was an austere wooded building left over from WW II. It had one room and a bathroom on the second floor. It was a real comedown from my room in Berlin. On the positive side, it had a Coke machine on the first floor.

###

On a Monday morning, I checked in for duty with the 12th Battle Group, 4th Infantry Division. The Battle Group consisted of four Infantry Companies, one Weapons Company, and a Headquarters Company. Each company had between 150-200 troops. I was assigned to the 4.2 Mortar Platoon within the Weapons Company. This weapon weighed 333 pounds and could be disassembled into three parts, with the heaviest part weighing 175 pounds. It had a range of 2.7 miles and each shell weighed 25 pounds. The upside was that each mortar required a three-quarter-ton truck for weapon and ammunition transportation. This meant I was able to ride. There was even enough space for a tent and heater on the truck.

After receiving my assignment, I started walking toward my company when I heard someone call out my name.

"Lieutenant Damrill, come over here."

I just checked in. Who would know me?

I turned, and there stood my first Company Commander from Berlin. I was surprised and responded,

"Captain Meyer, how are you? Whoops, you're a Major now. How are you, Major? What are you doing here?"

"I'm the Battle Group Operations Officer (S-3). I heard you're being assigned and when I saw you out my office window, I wanted to say hello. I tried to have you assigned to the S-3, but I didn't have any vacancies and Headquarters assigned you to Weapons Company. Don't worry, I have a vacancy coming up shortly and I'm going to have you fill that slot."

I responded, "That's great, you'll train me to be a staff officer, I'm looking forward to it."

"I see your parachute badge. Congratulations on finishing jump school. I've got someone waiting for me in the office. See you later."

"Yes sir."

This is going to be a great assignment.

The Operations Officer (S-3) is responsible for Battle Group training and field operation; of course, this is under the guidance of the Battle Group Commander.

###

I continued to my new company and checked in. According to my sketchy memory, the Platoon was commanded by a captain, a lieutenant in charge of the four 4.2 mortar Gun Section, a lieutenant in the Fire Control Center, and two lieutenants as Forward Observers. That was a lot of officers. I had just been a Weapons Platoon Leader in Berlin that had three 81mm mortars and two 106 recoilless anti-tank weapons. The 4.2 Mortars operated similar to the 81mm mortar, only bigger. I was assigned the gun section. This position wasn't very challenging. My task was to see that the mortars moved to the correct location, arrived with adequate ammunition, that was set up properly, and fired in the right direction. The biggest challenge when firing indirect weapons is to read a map and know your location. If shooting from the wrong position because you're lost, shells can land anywhere even landing on your own troops. There were no GPS's, and you had to determine your exact location by map and compass in large fields, deserts and mountains. Another common mistake is firing 180 degrees in the wrong direction.

###

Training in 1960 was 5 ½ days a week. On my first Saturday afternoon, I had the opportunity to explore Seattle and the University of Washington campus. Looking around campus, I ended up in the library and met a terrific-looking Swedish girl from Western University located in Bellingham, Washington. A town North of Seattle and just 30 miles from the Canadian border. She was working on her master's degree and decided to take some summer courses at the University of Washington. I couldn't believe my luck. We had several dates during the ensuing three weeks. The one most memorable date was an aquatic show on Green Lake in Seattle. The show could have been included in an Ester Williams swimming movie. Then we went on to the hydroplane boat races on Green Lake followed by the Seattle Seafair Parade. August is a big summer month for entertainment in Washington, which included festivals everywhere. But our dates soon ended as summer classes finished and she returned to Bellingham for the fall semester. She was stunning, but Bellingham was too far a drive for a date.

###

When I stayed in Seattle overnight, I went to a Navy base at Sand Point. It had been a seaplane base that had ceased operating as a seaplane base. There were still a few Navy activities on base which included an officer BOQ with an attached officers club.

###

After my first three weeks, my unit deployed for field maneuvers at Yakima Training Center in the center of Washington, or 150 miles east of Fort Lewis. The training was for two and one-half weeks. At the training center, we conducted field maneuvers and live fire exercises with our 4.2 mortars. Firing was routine, except, one time, when a shell was dropped down the tube, the propellant failed to explode. A call immediately rang out!

"Cease fire!"

It was now up to the crew to remove the defective round from the mortar tube. Carefully, they detached the tube from the base plate and then raised the tube high enough for the dud to slide out the open end. When it slides out, a crew member catches it around its center to avoid hitting the fuse tip. No words are spoken, and the rest of the platoon had moved rapidly to a safe distance. The mortar round has several fail-safe systems and it's a safe procedure. But it is a defective explosive and could have other defective parts. The soldier has essentially an unstable bomb in his hands.

Finally, all proceeded as planned; nerves calmed down, and the call rang out, "commence firing!"

Everything else was routine for the mortar platoon, except the months of August and September were unusually cold. No worries, the mortar platoon had heated tents.

###

There was one other incident in the Battle Group. One of our newly commissioned pilots was flying a single-engine, two-passenger L-19. His task was to take an artillery forward observer aloft so he could adjust artillery fire from the air. Returning from the mission, the pilot decided to give his passenger a short flying lesson. The purpose was to train the forward observer on procedures to follow should the pilot be hit by ground fire. He explained the aircraft would probably go into a spin and demonstrated how to handle the controls. The pilot thought he had the altitude for this maneuver, but forgot he was not at sea level and didn't adjust for the increased ground elevation; therefore, crashing into a hillside killing his passenger. The pilot suffered head injuries and was despondent because he had killed his passenger. He realized that this incident and his head injury might end both his flying and military career.

###

It's not unusual to have a few people killed during maneuvers. Keep in mind that tanks, artillery, mortars, and machine guns are being operated and fired by teenagers and twenty-year-olds. In addition, these young soldiers are the pilots, tank, and truck drivers, that operate and maintain these vehicles. Many of these young soldiers have a level of responsibility equivalent to forty-year- old civilians.

After maneuvers, the weather was excellent, and I was invited to go fishing for salmon in the Puget Sound next to Fort Lewis. I liked being on the water but didn't care much for fishing. I bought a cheap fishing pole and, after an hour on the water, I conveniently let it fall overboard, making it look like an accident. Those onboard yelled out, "Lieutenant Damrill your fishing pole fell overboard,"

"Damn it, I wasn't paying attention, and it slipped out of my hand. I must have had a bite, and it took my pole."

Everyone laughed hilariously and said how sorry they were that my fishing was over for the day. I spent the rest of the afternoon enjoying the sun on the water coupled with the good company on board.

It was also football season, and I attended several of the University of Washington football games. They had a great season and played in the Rose Bowl on New Year's Day in 1961 and won over Minnesota's Golden Gophers 17 to 7.

CHAPTER 25.

A month after returning from maneuvers, I was called by Major Meyers (S-3).

"Lieutenant Damrill, I have orders for you to transfer to the S-3 tomorrow."

"You did it! I'm on my way now."

I was delighted to be out of the mortar platoon. There was not much action there. Little did I realize how busy the S-3 staff was, and it would take several weekends to understand the new assignment which included, as an additional task, being Air Control Officer. If we required fighter airplane support, my job was to direct them to the target. My training from my boss was:

"Lieutenant Damrill there's your jeep loaded with radios, learn how to use them so you can talk to the pilots. Oh, by the way, here are a couple of manuals to look at."

This is a great job, look at all those radios!

Fortunately, the Air Force had the primary job of directing targets and I was backup. Usually, when you went to the field for exercises, an Air Force pilot was attached with his jeep full of radios. If he didn't show, or if we had to split up to cover a larger area, I would have the job.

After I was on my new job for two months, I had learned the job well enough to take off both Saturday afternoon and Sunday. Up to this point, I was taking only Saturday afternoon off to go to University of Florida football games. On an army post in the United States, you are separated from the civilian community, and it's hard to meet people off-post socially. Most local girls are not that excited about possibly leaving their hometown for a vagabond life in the military. Stymied, and looking for some type of activity, I decided to try snow skiing. Just 65 miles to the east was Snoqualmie Pass. However, it offered only daytime skiing and had few overnight activities. After a couple of trips, I began to notice that those skiing appeared to be from upper-income families, educated, and adventurous. Ski equipment, clothing, lifts, and transportation were not cheap. Most skiers had a BMI (Body Mass Index) of 24, not overweight; probably, since they tended to be athletic anyway. For those who didn't meet all the requirements, they were at least adventurists. Also, I noticed that introductions were easy. On the second trip, a girl accidentally collided with me at the bottom of a slope. Well, I'm not sure it was an accident. Girls have their own method of introduction.

After the collision, a breathless voice said, "Are you okay?"

"Sure, how about you?"

'I'm okay, sorry I ran into you, but I lost control of my skies."

"Say, I think it's time for a break. How about going for a Martini or hot chocolate?"

"Great timing, what are we waiting for?" she gushed.

###

We enjoyed the Martini's. During the discussion, she said she was an airline stewardess, stationed out of Seattle. We agreed to meet in Seattle the following weekend for dinner.

###

The next weekend I picked her up and explained,

"I have a couple of places in mind, do you have anywhere special you would like to go?"

Her eyes lit up what this offer of a choice.

"I know just the place.".

We pulled up in front of an exclusive and quite costly nightclub. A parking attendant quickly took charge of my car, a doorman opened the door. We headed inside. I was wearing a casual sports coat and tie but noticed those entering were extremely better dressed. With my sports coat, I was underdressed for the occasion and felt out of place. Inside my date immediately ran into friends. As I was being introduced, I noticed there was some hesitation on their part as I was asked questions; some inquiries were rather rude, "Do they pay much in the military?"

"Have you killed anyone?"

At first, when people are introduced, new acquaintances are just trying to make conversation. This was not the case for these discussions. They were outwardly hostile.

"I Haven't assassinated anyone here yet; it is tempting."

After my equally insulting reply, I was ignored. I had to contain my surge of anger, but then I noticed a group of mixed ages and genders having a good time near a piano player. I wandered over to check it out and was greeted with open arms.

"We heard loud- mouth over there," don't just stand there, join us," the pianist called out.

"Thanks, I will."

"Is this your first run-in with the anti-military trust- baby brats of Seattle?" he murmured.

I nodded and was now an accepted member of the piano group. After a couple of drinks, there was developing one of those magical moments when everyone in the group connected for an exceptionally good time.

Then my date reappeared and with a slight look of embarrassment on her face said,

"Oh, there you are. I have been looking all over for you. Can we go now, I have a flight in the morning?"

What happened? My initial impression of her fantastically alluring appeal had disappeared.

I was having a good time and didn't want to separate from the group, but I reluctantly replied, "Sure, let's go."

I was somewhat disappointed that hadn't measured up to her expectations, but it was okay. It was obvious that I couldn't afford to take her out. I had to give her credit; she had quickly checked out my financial status. It took me a month to recover financially from the expense of that date.

###

In November 1960, I got a card from a 1st Lieutenant I had known in Berlin, Germany. He was the one who had escorted a USO group through Europe for two months and married one of the performers, and when he had returned to the company, was dissatisfied with the new company commander and semi-seriously, wanted me to join him in deposing the commander if we became evolved in a shooting war with Russia. In the letter, he invited me to visit him and his wife on New Year's at the Presidio in the Monterey Annex. This is the location of the Defense Language Institute Foreign Language Center, which is near Carmel, California. He had been assigned to the language Institute for one year to learn how to speak, read, and write in Chinese. I accepted.

###

Next to Fort Lewis was McChord Air Force Base, which provided the opportunity to sign up for "Space Available" free seats on out- going flights. I was in luck, there was a transport plane heading to Travis Air Force Base, California with seats available; and was near Carmel. We took off in the usual morning fog and rain, and after a few minutes, we were above the clouds in the sunlight. It is hard to describe how great it was to see the sun, after two months of dismal Washington weather. Landing at Travis AFB, I rented a car; and shortly thereafter, arrived at my friend's apartment. He heard the car pull up in the driveway, then he and his wife were in the doorway waving. He shouted out a warm greeting,

"Hi Ron, you made it." His wife chimed in,

"Haven't seen you since Berlin," he directed let me show you to your room and then we can have some cocktails."

After an evening of conversation, drinks, and snacks, we were ready to turn in for the night.

In closing, my friend said, "We're going to Carmel Beach tomorrow, and we will pick up your date on the way. For New Years, we will all be going to the officers club."

"Wow, this visit includes a girl! See you in the morning."

###

The next morning, we picked up a cute girl, who greeted me,

"Hi, I've been looking forward to meeting you."

Nice looking for a blind date. Hope she thinks the same.

"What a great day for the beach, look at all that sun. Thanks, for coming along."

###

We spent a lot of time on the beach and in the evenings visited the restaurants in Carmel, ending with New Year's Eve at the officers club. This was one of my best vacations.

###

On my return, I was unable to find a military flight and caught a train. When I boarded, I felt I was on the' Rose Bowl Express' to Seattle.

The train was packed with University of Washington students returning from the Rose Bowl football game. I found a seat and after a time, the person seated next to me left. And as soon as the seat was vacant a nice-looking girl sat down and said,

"I'm lucky to get this seat, can I sit next to you?"

I glanced around,

There were a few other vacant seats.

"Glad for the company, what did you think of the game?"

"Did you go to the game?"

"No, I was on the beach in Carmel."

"Are you going back to the University?'

"No, I'm getting off in Tacoma, I'm a Lieutenant in the Army at Fort Lewis."

She looks interested.

After 30 minutes of conversation, I asked,

"How about meeting you Saturday afternoon, at that popular bookstore off campus, and we'll look the city over."

"Well okay, I'll be there at one o'clock."

She departed with a smile on her face. She went to the Rose Bowl game and met a stranger on the Rose Bowl Express who would meet her on Saturday. She had scored.

###

On Saturday I arrived a few minutes early and promptly at one o'clock she was there. I said,

Hi, I have a great idea. I've reserved a seaplane and pilot who will fly us around Seattle and Puget Sound for an hour."

"I've never been up in an airplane. I'm not sure about this?"

There were several seaplane bases within three miles of the University.

"Never been up in an airplane! You'll have a great time. It's fabulous."

Reluctantly, she said, "Okay."

In 15 minutes, we arrived at the seaplane base and met the pilot of a small four-place seaplane. As we boarded I had my date sit in the Co-pilot's seat.

She's fascinated by all in instruments in the cockpit. This is going to be okay.

There was a slight wind, and the bay had some protection from the wind and the water was smooth. As we taxied for the take off the pilot was talking to my date through our headsets, explaining what he was doing. As we taxied, the plane was rocking slightly on small waves. From the back seat, I noticed my date's hands were starting to grip the sides of her seat. After taking off and reaching an altitude of 2,000 feet, the wind became more noticeable, and the plane rocked and bumped in the rough air. My date was now tightly gripping her seat and was turning pale. Speaking over the headset, she almost shouted,

"Take me back, I don't feel good."

The pilot responded, "We'll land immediately."

When we landed, my date exited the plane rapidly and headed for a hidden place on the dock and proceeded to get sick. Finally, she reappeared, and I asked, "How are you doing?"

"Take me back to the university. "There was no conversation on the return trip. When we arrived at the bookstore, she jumped out, slammed the door, and was gone. That was the last date I had for several months.

CHAPTER 26.

It was January 1961 and time for the Battle Group Field Tactical Exercise (FTX) test. Accompanying the Battle Group were umpires responsible for both controlling and grading the performance of the Battle Group in a tactical field environment.

###

Before deployment, I was joined by an Air Force Forward Air Controller (FAC) for the coordination of air strikes. The times of these air strikes were well established in the exercise scenarios. When I wasn't busy assisting in controlling aircraft, I was given an additional task as a Liaison officer. The job was to visit higher, adjacent, and lower headquarters to deliver tactical written orders that were too lengthy to be transmitted over radios or teletype. Once delivered, I would wait till the orders were read and understood, and answer questions as necessary. Additionally, I would review their tactical maps to ensure data posted on their maps correlated with information on Battle Group maps.

###

The first day we simulated replacing a unit in a defensive position that had several casualties. During this replacement period, the aggressors (enemy) attempted to launch an attack to take advantage of the confusion created during the relief operation. We used our close air support capability to defeat the enemy attack. Finally, in control of our front lines, we consolidated and prepared for a second attack. We sent out patrols to try and determine the enemy's intentions. Patrols reported the enemy had built up a massive force for their second assault. Confronted with overwhelming odds, we conducted a night withdrawal to a secondary defensive position. We left a small mobile covering force on our old position to convince the enemy that it was still occupied, thus allowing the main body to conduct an organized withdrawal. This maneuver disguised our new relocation causing the enemy to commit its full force of men and resources to attack a non-occupied position. The covering force would later withdraw before they became closely engaged. Usually, the enemy needs to regroup after taking an objective. However, should the opposing force have the capability to continue the attack, the mobile covering force slows them down and disrupts their advances using delaying tactics, such as relocating to successive defensive positions. They would hold this position just long enough to force the enemy to deploy for an assault. This maneuver takes time. As soon as the enemy prepared to attack their position, they would withdraw to another location nearby.

###

The enemy attacked, and our covering force withdrew while our artillery fire saturated our old position the enemy had taken. The enemy was now in disarray, and we prepared to launch a counterattack. To assist in our mobility, we planned to lift one company by helicopter through a weak point in their air defenses. This assault would bypass or overfly the front lines and attack air support weapons (artillery) and their supply depots.

###

Our reserve company was selected for the helicopter assault. The reserves were issued a warning order, by coded radio message, to be prepared to move out on short notice. Further information was to follow. As Liaison Officer, I was ordered to carry the written orders to "D" Company and present them to the company commander at 8:00 a.m. and not before.

I was accompanied by an umpire who was to grade the company's execution of the order. The helicopter tactical air lift was to start at 8:00 a.m. and the umpire stayed with me to ensure the company didn't receive the orders until 8:00 a.m.

###

The umpire and I arrived at 7:30 a.m. I couldn't believe what I am observing. The troops were still in sleeping bags and equipment was scattered everywhere. The Company Commander was having a cup of coffee. I walked over and said, "Sir, did you get the warning order to be prepared to move out?"

The company commander replied, "Lieutenant, it's none of your concern. But, for your information, we can easily move out in a couple of minutes."

Unbelievable! It will take an hour to get this group moving.

This wouldn't have happened in a Berlin unit.

Then the umpire grabbed me and took me to a quiet spot.

"Lieutenant Damrill, you're giving out too much information. You say anything else, and I'll stop the exercise."

After our initial conversation, the Company Commander continued to ignore us. I thought our presence would have alerted him that an action was about to take place.

At 8:00 a.m. in the presence of the umpire, I took the orders over to the Company Commander and quickly told him the contents. "You are to be picked up by helicopters at 9:00 a.m. at a location 40 minutes by foot. Captain, can you make it?"

"Damn it Lieutenant, why didn't you tell me sooner."

Hell, you had a warning order, I was almost waving the written order in your face and an umpire was with me. Where was your head?

Again, I was surprised, the company showed no urgency and was moving in slow motion. Again, to speed up the operation, I said to the commander, "Sir, do you think you can make the pickup time?"

"No problem, they'll just have to wait until we get there."

What's he thinking about?

The umpire (a senior Major) heard our conversation and was closely observing the action of the troops, who were making only slow progress.

###

When we arrived at the helicopter pick-up landing zone, the helicopters were gone. In a combat zone, helicopters are extremely vulnerable to enemy fire. They land just long enough for troops to load.

###

The Battle Group Commander met us as we arrived. He wasn't happy.

"Captain, you're relieved of duty! You have two hours to report to the division for reassignment!"

###

The exercise was over, and everyone returned to the barracks. Two weeks later "D" Company received its annual Inspector General (I.G.) Inspection. Almost every unit in the Army has an annual I.G. inspection. The overall purpose is to ensure every unit is being run according to established regulations. They check accountability and maintenance of equipment, ensure administrative records are correct and the dining facility provides proper nutrition and well-cooked food for the troops. Finally, the status on troop morale was evaluated.

###

Company "D" failed the inspection in every category. Though the company commander had been relieved, the Executive Officer and First Sergeant should have been able to achieve a satisfactory rating. The inspection was announced weeks in advance and was not a surprise. To make matters worse the Executive Officer, who was responsible for managing money in the Unit fund, was caught borrowing (stealing) from the fund. As a result, he was forced to resign from the Army.

A Unit fund is established in most military units. This fund is given a hundred or more dollars a month, to be used to enhance troop morale. For example, the money can be used for a unit party or buying a TV for the company Day Room.

###

Company "D" had hit bottom. They caused the Battle Group to fail its annual field test, and the company commander was relieved. It failed its annual I.G. inspection and the Executive Officer was forced to resign for stealing money from the Unit Fund. No one had ever heard of a company achieving such a poor record.

###

As a result, the remaining company officers and First Sergeant were reassigned. The following day a new Company Commander was assigned.

The same day, my boss in the S-3 (Operations Officer) said, "Lieutenant Damrill, the Battle Group Commander wants you in his office immediately."

"What's up?"

"Not sure, but I think you're being reassigned."

This doesn't look good. What's going on?

###

Two minutes later, I'm in the Headquarters.

"I heard the Colonel wants to see me."

I hardly got these words out of my mouth, "Lieutenant Damrill, reporting, Sir."

"I'm assigning you to Company "D" as Executive Officer."

I inadvertently blurted out, **"D" Company."**

The worst unit on post

Just the mention of Company 'D" brought anger to his face. He went on to say, "I need someone over there I can count on and who has the experience, the new company commander is an aviator with little ground experience." "Yes Sir."

I started to depart, and the Colonel made one last comment, Lieutenant Damrill, turn that company around!"

"Yes Sir."

Me, turn the company around?

###

What the Colonel meant by the new Company Commander, is that aviation didn't have its own branch of service in the 1960s. To fill the aviation slots, pilots were borrowed from the infantry, artillery, armor, and other branches. For the pilots to keep current in their basic branch, they were required to return to their branch every fourth year. The new company commander had probably been on ground duty one year as a Lieutenant and spent the rest of his time flying. The second problem is aviators are more lenient, something this company did not need.

###

After seeing the Colonel, I immediately proceeded to company "D" and reported to the new company commander. I knocked on his office door and entered.

"Lieutenant Damrill reporting for duty."

"I heard you were coming, sit down and let's talk."

As we talked, he immediately eased into all my duty responsibilities. Usually, the Executive Officer's duties are enough. By the time the discussion was over, I was the Executive Officer, Weapons Platoon Leader, Motor Officer, Training Officer, and responsible for the Unit Fund. This was the aviator's approach to assigning tasks.

I had to give him credit, he gave me the right jobs. As Weapons Platoon Leader, I had direct access to troops that I could use for other tasks. The platoon had most of the vehicles and the soldiers were responsible for maintenance. Best of all, I was the Motor Officer with direct control of motor maintenance personnel. I even controlled the training schedule so I could prioritize. Division training is conducted on an annual cycle, but there is enough free time allocated for flexibility.

Had the Colonel talked to him about the purpose of my assignment?

###

It was the end of the day, and I sat down at my desk in my own office. My first office since I had been commissioned. I sat there long after duty hours outlining, in my mind, what actions I should take. We had six weeks to get ready for reinspection. A month after the inspection, we were scheduled for our company field test. Troop morale was low. Any time the soldiers left the company area, and it was discovered they were from Company "D," they would be the object of, not so friendly, harassment. With the little free time they would now have, they would not have so much negative feedback.

###

Subconsciously, I felt the only way these tasks could be accomplished in this short time was to develop the personality of a ruthless Marine Corps Drill Instructor (D.I.). The company commander could show outward calm and certainty of a positive outcome for the upcoming evaluation while I went to work to ensure that that happened.

I could succeed or fail in this new position. I liked the challenge of adventuring into the unknown. To get started, I needed to begin practicing my new split personality (Marine D.I.), to shock the company back into being successful in the Army. This will be fun, and a new adventure.

CHAPTER 27.

I sat down at my desk and started laying out a timeline of tasks to be accomplished. First was the I.G. inspection in five weeks, followed one month later by our annual field test. After determining my first action to be taken on the following day, there was a knock on my door.

It was after-duty hours, who could that be?

There stood one of the company's lieutenants who was clearing post because he had been fired, among other things, due to the failed field test. I opened the conversation with, "How are you doing? Did you leave something behind?"

He responded, "I heard you are the new Training Officer, and as the previous Training Officer, I signed for some aggressor (enemy) uniforms from Post Training Aids. I need to have someone sign for the uniforms before they let me leave the post. It's late, but could you sign for them?"

"You're transferring a year and one-half before normal rotation for officers on an accompanied tour (with family) in the United States is three years."

He explained, "I know, I've been assigned to Korea for one year on an unaccompanied assignment (without family). I must get my wife relocated near her parents before I leave for Korea."

When a soldier has an unaccompanied assignment longer than six months, he is required to move his family off post. Families often choose to relocate near or with the wife's parents.

Replying I started, "That's unusual, your wife must be furious. Say, what really happened in D Company?" I prodded.

"I'm not totally sure myself and I've been instructed not to talk about anything concerning the company."

Was he instructed to not talk about anything, or was he refusing to tell me?

"Sure, I'll be glad to help. Let's get it done."

"This way," he stated, "I have them in the training room."

I was surprised to see that there were only ten uniforms present and setting beside them were receipts for twenty more.

He said, "These receipts are for the other twenty uniforms signed out to troops in the company."

The receipts looked legitimate. I counted the uniforms and receipts and signed all thirty uniforms. Wrong! This was my mistake. Never sign for anything unless you can confirm their existence, see, and touch the items. Again, I assumed he was honest. I should have reminded myself, for some unclear complication, he had just been relieved of duty.

###

The next morning, I called in the Training NCO and asked him to take the receipts and go collect the uniforms from the receipt holders. Then we would turn in the thirty uniforms. A few minutes later he returned and said, with an embarrassed look on his face, "These receipts are old and the persons who signed them out are no longer in the unit."

Damn it, how could I be so gullible. Looks like I will have to pay for them, probably a month's pay.

No wonder he was fired. What else will I have to rectify? Command had reassigned him to one of the least desirable posts in the Army, perhaps as a punishment.

"Sergeant, gather up the uniforms and let's turn in what we have."

###

Arriving at Division Training Aids, I told the civilian working there, "I have only ten of the thirty uniforms. Unfortunately, I signed them for the previous Training Officer. I suppose I will have to pay for the others?"

"Don't worry lieutenant, I'll write off the missing twenty as ruined during field exercises. It happens."

I couldn't believe it, the sergeant with me had a stunned look of disbelief on his face.

"Thanks, that's a relief."

When we left, the sergeant commented, "I can't believe he gave you credit for that many missing uniforms, that's never been my previous experience."

"I'm surprised too," I replied with relief, 'let's go over to the I.G. Office and ask them what we need to do to pass our I.G. inspection."

Sir, you can't do that."

"I know; nevertheless, let's see what happens?"

###

When we arrived at the I.G. Office, a senior NCO was sitting behind the desk.

"I'm from Company D- 12th Battle Group, we are due for a re-inspection next month. Can you give us any guidance?"

"I know all about your company. Sure, here are the checklists we use. We encourage you to use them. We want units to pass; if they follow the checklists, they will be up to Army standards. That's our goal and good luck."

Oh no, our derelict company is known by everyone. I might as well push for all the help I can get while he is in a cooperative mood.

"Thanks, can I have two copies?"

"No problem, we will see you for re-inspection in a month."

My sergeant couldn't believe it was so easy to get assistance, neither could I. When we returned to the company, the sergeant exaggerated our visits. He was relaying how I had convinced Training Aids that they should accept the fact the aggressor uniforms were destroyed in training, giving us credit for turning in thirty uniforms. He also conveyed how I talked the I.G. into giving us their inspection checklists. He left out how easy it was. Nevertheless, I appreciated his support in increasing my reputation within the company.

###

After checking with the company commander, I called key personnel in for a meeting and gave each person the checklists pertaining to their area of inspection. There were different lists for the motor pool, mess hall, platoons, and others. I informed them that, "You will have several pre-I.G. inspections using these lists starting in one week."

Upon completion, and as everyone was leaving, I called the Motor Pool NCO over and requested, "Take me to the motor pool and show me what you have."

"Yes Sir."

###

As we were walking over, the Motor Sargent explained, "The motor pool is completely ignored by the company, we have little assistance, and it will be impossible to get ready for the reinspection."

Arriving at the motor pool. I immediately saw what he meant. Many vehicles were poorly maintained, and the place was a general mess. It reminded me of my failing taxi company in Fort Scott, Kansas. We talked for a while, and because I had just completed the Motor Officer Course, I understood his language.

I replied, "I see your problem. I'll bring you a sergeant and six men tomorrow morning from the Weapons Platoon. They will be directly assigned for your assistance."

###

The next morning, there I was, with one NCO and six men to be assigned to the motor pool. There were two for paperwork, two for maintenance, and two to keep the vehicles clean with proper fluids and air in all the tires. The NCO was to supervise them as directed by the Motor Sergeant.

I told the Motor Sergeant, "Here are your men, put them to work. Also, I noticed your spare parts shelves are empty, I know you have requested parts, but they won't arrive before inspection. Send your people out to borrow parts and fill the shelves. Inspectors don't like to see empty shelves. To them, it shows requests haven't been submitted in a timely manner. Fill them by the end of next week."

The sergeant was a sharp guy and was delighted that someone was finally supporting him. I went to the motor pool daily and conducted spot inspections. One technique was to go to the motor pool before the duty day started and let some air out of the tire of a specific vehicle, then I would return to the Motor Pool at nine o'clock. If the two soldiers responsible for that vehicle found the error, all was good. As things improved, I began to commend them at their workplace and throughout the company.

###

The I.G. Inspections I had in Berlin, had given me valuable experience. My next visit was to the orderly room and training room.

Again, there were few Army regulations or training manuals on the shelves. Both the First Sergeant and Training NCO were present as I brought the empty shelves to their attention.

"We need an office with all required regulations and manuals for reference. We can't function without them. The goal is to have one hundred percent present and fully visible by the end of next week. I'll assign one additional sergeant to each section to get the job done. If those sergeants are smart, they will get men from their squad to assist."

###

Two days later, the NCO in charge of training came into my office and reported, "The NCO, you gave me to scrounge for manuals, is just taking an extended coffee break. He is gone all morning. When he returns, he says he couldn't locate any manuals. I tell him where to look, but he doesn't do it, I checked."

Time for me to go into my Marine Corps Drill Instructor personality.

"First Sergeant, get the NCO assigned to the training section, his platoon leader, and platoon sergeant in my office at one o'clock."

###

At one o'clock, there stood the dud sergeant, a new Second Lieutenant, and a junior Platoon Sergeant. I went into my D.I. impersonation and bellowed, "This dud of a sergeant you sent me, is weaseling out of his duty, spending all morning goofing off and not doing his job. This gold brick is refusing to work for the Training NCO. Lieutenant, you sent me the worst NCO in your platoon. Platoon sergeant, it is your duty to train your Second Lieutenant not to do dumb things. Since I can't count on you to provide responsible soldiers, Lieutenant, you will oversee getting the manuals. Your Platoon Sergeant and that deadbeat standing next to you are your assistants. On my desk, I have typed letters of reprimand. If the three of you don't have these shelves full in one week, with the enthusiastic help of that lazy sergeant standing between you, I'm forwarding the letters to personnel to be placed in your records. If you, Second Lieutenant want to make First Lieutenant, and your Platoon Sergeant wants to make First Sergeant, those shelves need to be full in a week. Lieutenant, is that low-life NCO standing next to you on Proficiency Pay?"

"I don't know, sir."

"You tell him, if he is, he had better be prepared to tell his wife that he is about to lose his proficiency pay if shelves are not filled in one week."

I noticed the sergeant's face turned pale.

Wife was the magic word.

I was bluffing, I didn't have the authority for such action, nor would I have done it. However, they could not be sure of this.

###

My office was next to the Company Commander, the door was always open. He, and half the company, were listening in. I guess they knew something was up and they had gathered around down the hall. Afterward, the Company Commander grinned, "That was quite a show, do you think you'll get results? Was that a little rough?"

I wasn't sure what he meant. Does he mean, will my experiment work? In retrospect, this was an aviator reprimand. It was so benign, I believed he was reluctantly agreeing. It was true, I arrived with the force of a 'lightning bolt'. This was not a popular position, but something had to be done. I remember the Battle Group Commander saying, "Lieutenant Damrill turn this company around."

###

CHAPTER 28.

One week later, the shelves weren't full, but the lieutenant and his assistants were hustling. They must have had the whole platoon on the project. I didn't say anything, I knew it would be almost impossible to find all the required publications.

###

I put on a couple more theatrical productions of my irate drill instructor. After that, everyone started to pull together, looked excited, and appeared to be developing a sense of pride associated with doing a good job.

###

Another platoon was responsible for the day room (recreation area). They became so interested that it began to look like someone's living room. I wasn't sure and didn't ask questions, but I believe some of the furniture was on loan from senior NCOs' homes.

###

Now, I had to get the unit fund in order. I stayed after duty hours and came in on weekends to make the books ready for audit. I had a business degree and several accounting courses. The books were simple, especially with the illustrated instructions from the I.G., almost as simple as a child's picture book. The biggest problem was locating all the bills, receipts of payment, deposit slips and bank statements. This was such a small task; I couldn't understand why it had so much prominence in the inspection, then I recalled that the last lieutenant in charge of the fund had been caught stealing some of the money and was forced to resign or be court-martialed. While I was putting the fund together, I had an idea, I'll establish a unit fund committee to suggest how funds will be spent, and they will monitor its operation. I'll request each platoon to send a representative. This should discourage any dishonest operations of the fund and give the troops some control over their area. Two weeks had gone by when I heard the battle group commander had been reassigned. Had he been replaced because of the failed field test or because he had served his allotted time in command?

###

Our new battle group commander arrived a week later. We had a battle group officers' call where he introduced himself and gave us a short speech. When I saw him, I noticed he was only a Lieutenant Colonel (LTC) and not a full Colonel. He was assigned from the Pentagon and looked more like a politician than a commander. Accompanying him was a thin, short, tough-looking major, who looked like he was looking for a fight of any kind. He was to be his executive officer and was to handle any problems the battle group might encounter. It was clear if there was a problem, you saw the executive officer for resolution. All anyone knew about the new executive officer was he had come from Fort Bragg, North Carolina. Fort Bragg has the 82nd Airborne Division, Special Forces, and several specialized units to conduct clandestine missions. He had left his family behind in post-housing. This meant he was on a six-month assignment. If longer, he would have had to move his family off post.

###

Back in the company, the training was organized to have an I.G. inspection rehearsal starting every Friday at one o'clock through Saturday noon. This would be a barracks inspection, with the troops standing by their bunks with all their military clothing and equipment for inspection. First, the platoon leaders would inspect using their checklists. Second, the company commander would inspect. My weapons platoon was inspected first. After inspection, I would proceed ahead of the company commander to the mess hall, supply room, training room, communication room, and motor pool to make sure they were prepared. Enough time was allocated between inspections to correct deficiencies before the company commander's inspection. This lasted three weekends. During this period, the senior NCOs began to take an interest. The first couple of weeks they just watched.

It looked like they were thinking, "is this a quick splash? Would the officers revert to the lackadaisical leadership of the previous commanders?"

They noticed that the new leadership continued to strive for excellence, and they joined in.

###

The big day arrived, and the I.G. inspection team was greeted and guided to the day room where coffee and donuts were made available. Playing in the background was soft patriotic music. You could see the amazement on their faces as they gazed at the day room decorations. The chief inspector, plus two of his inspectors, company commander and I went to the commander's office for a brief discussion before formal inspection began.

Before entering the commander's office, one of the inspectors called me aside and said,

"Show me your unit fund books."

My office was located next to the commander's office.

"This way. These are the books on my desk, and this is my enlisted committee that monitors the income and spending." I proceeded to introduce the committee by name, giving them recognition.

The inspector sat down and looked at the books for a few seconds, quickly checking a few specific figures. Then he abruptly stood up and said to the chief inspector in the next room, "Come and look at these books."

My heart stopped for a second.

What could be wrong?

As the Chief stood at my desk looking at the books, his inspector said, "I can't believe it, the figures are correct, and the books are laid out exactly as directed in our regulations. Lieutenant Damrill also has a committee to review income and expenses. This doesn't happen often. By the way, this is the officer who picked up our checklists. That doesn't happen often either."

They glanced through the door into the orderly room, and another inspector exclaimed, "Look at the shelves full of regulations and manuals."

Everyone's face changed from a tense to a relaxed smile.

I could see they were thinking that maybe the company would pass. These were seasoned inspectors and knew requisitions for regulations and manuals couldn't have been filled that quickly from the last inspection. They didn't ask questions and were impressed by the company's effort.

###

The company commander escorted the chief inspector to check the troops in the barracks and other areas in the company building. I returned to the day room and joined the inspectors for the motor pool. In the motor pool, the drivers were standing by their vehicles and excitedly waiting to be inspected. This gave the soldiers a sense of pride and proprietorship. They answered the inspectors' questions freely. The inspectors were pleased with the response and enjoyed talking to everyone. I noticed when they did find a deficiency, the driver showed interest in how it should be corrected. Because of this relationship, I noticed the inspectors weren't writing them up.

###

The inspection was over in less than four hours and was a success. The company received a high score, and all was good. Now the next three weeks will be rehearsing for the field training test.

###

In the 1960s, field tests for companies usually had the following scenarios: the company starts the exercise by moving to an assembly area, followed by orders to occupy a defensive position. While in position, the enemy penetrates the company's front line, forcing the company commander to counterattack with his reserve platoon to restore his stance. Enemy forces continued to build up which forced a night withdrawal to either another defensive position or to an assembly area behind friendly lines. The following morning the company attacks with force to destroy the enemy.

###

While escorting an umpire to Company D, during the battle group test, I remembered how slowly the previous Company D commander responded to field movement orders. Using radio communications still takes a few minutes to disseminate information.

There must be a faster way.

I remember from my training in Berlin how effective flares were to communicate a coordinated, fast response. I made this recommendation to the commander. He agreed, and we used this tactic during our practice field tests. For example, if you had to counter-attack in the defensive position, there would be one red flare to counter to the left, two to the middle, and three to the right. For the withdrawal, two white flares would be fired simultaneously, or in other situations, it meant you were moving in five minutes. Flare communication codes would change periodically if you were in the field for an extended period or combat.

###

After three weeks of rehearsal, the day of the field exercise was about to begin. Early in the morning, we were alerted to deploy to the field and given map coordinates to the assembly area. The company commander departed for headquarters to receive orders for the exercise while I took the company to the designated assembly area. I occupied the lead vehicle in our column when we arrived at our designated location. Looking around the area, I noticed, off to my right, a jeep pulled out of a concealed position and headed in my direction. On the front of the jeep was a large license plate showing one star.

What's a general doing here? I've never seen a general checking training.

In a division, you have a major general as division commander (2 stars), and two brigadier generals as assistant division commanders (1 star). One brigadier supervises training and the other overlooks logistics. Approaching was the brigadier general of training.

Was he checking up on the notorious Company "D" or just checking on training?

I came to a stop in my jeep to greet the general and signaled to the first sergeant to continue and set up the assembly area as we had rehearsed. I reported, "Lieutenant Damrill, Executive Officer of Company D, sir.

The general looks disappointed I didn't stop the whole column.

"Lieutenant, who's in charge? Where is the column going?"

"I am, the company commander is at headquarters receiving orders for our field test. The troops are moving into their assembly area. They know what to do."

He looks disappointed that I'm not shouting out commands.

The Brigadier knew what training was being conducted and started quizzing me on the organization of the assembly area. It appeared he was going down the field manual checklist for this tactical maneuver. As he asked the questions, I would point to the units that were physically putting into action the question he had asked about. He could see it happening as he spoke.

He seems disappointed that I have a positive answer for all his questions. I won't answer the next one.

"Lieutenant, where are your outposts?"

"Good point sir, I'll double-check on it."

He's smiling, he must have approved.

"Carry on lieutenant, no wait a minute." He paused and looked at my name tag. "Carry on, Lieutenant Damrill."

I drove over to a nearby platoon that had the task of sending out an observation post. As I arrived, the men for the observation post were just leaving. From the general's view, it looked like I had followed his suggestion, and he could see the men departing on their mission. He watched a few more minutes and departed.

It is advisable to take advantage of opportunities to have your superiors display positively. It may be beneficial for you as well. In other words, make the boss look good, and he will be inclined to make you look good. Also, reading emotional responses can be very helpful, if accurate!

###

The remainder of the exercise was well executed by the company commander. Finally, the exercise was over, and the company moved to a non-tactical area. The mess truck was there, and the soldiers had breakfast in the field. I did notice that the umpires were hanging around. Usually, they leave when the exercise is over.

Were they staying for breakfast with the troops? Was there to be an unannounced debrief after breakfast? What's going on?

The troops finished breakfast and were lying around with their equipment off. Some were congratulating themselves on the exercise, and others were taking a nap after being up all night.

The transportation taking us back to the barracks was delayed. I noticed the general driving up in his jeep and engaging the company commander in conversation.

As I stood next to my jeep with the first sergeant, one of the umpires approached and said, “The exercise has been extended.”

“What? You’re kidding?”

“I’m serious, you’re to be at this location on the map in one hour.”

The first sergeant overheard the conversation and gave out a shout to the troops, “Put on your gear, we’re moving out.”

The men responded, “You’re joking, the exercise is over.”

I had my driver grab two white flares from the jeep and fire them. This was the emergency signal to move out in five minutes. The men immediately responded to the flares. I sent my driver to inform the company commander, who was still talking to the general. We were on the road in ten minutes. Since this was a helicopter lift, the vehicles and drivers were left behind to secure the rear area and clean up any debris left.

The umpires are enjoying themselves. They are not grading.

Is this part of the test or is the general just curious about our ability to move quickly?

During the last battle group field test, I had escorted the umpire, who was evaluating company D during their mission to conduct an air assault maneuver using helicopters. The company had reacted slowly and missed their helicopter pick-up time during the battlegroup field test. This time, we arrived 15 minutes early and instead of helicopters, there were 2 ½ ton trucks there waiting to transport us back to our barracks. The umpires and general were all smiling. We had successfully passed the I.G. inspection and our field test.

CHAPTER 29.

I left the `company area at about 7:00 P.M. and went to the casual infantry officers' club. Casual meant you could wear fatigues. This club was an annex of the main officers' club and was located near the field units. I would go for my daily, evening diet of beer and potato chips topped with sliced dill pickles. I might have a hamburger later in the evening. Major Badowski, Battle Group Executive Officer also dropped by about the same time since he was unaccompanied, and his wife was at Fort Bragg. We became friends and since he met me, he became interested in Company D's progress. After the company was successful in passing its I.G. inspection and field test, he said he had a special project for me and that my company commander would inform me to report to him tomorrow for the project. The next morning Captain Davies, the Company Commander took me aside and said,

"The Battle Group has a special assignment for you, and you are to report to Major Badowski for instructions."

"Yes sir, any idea what they want?"

"No clue."

###

I proceeded to group headquarters and reported to the executive officer, "Lieutenant Damrill reporting for assignment, sir."

He responded, "I've assigned you as Special Court-Martial Trial Counsel for an upcoming case."

What's so special about being a trial counsel?

He continued, "A bullying wise guy struck his squad leader and knocked him out. After the incident, two tough senior NCOs grabbed the private and took him to the woods. In the woods, and out of sight, the NCOs proceeded to rough up the private who had struck a junior NCO. When they finished providing NCO discipline, the soldier had to be evacuated to the hospital. Unfortunately, there had to be an explanation of how the injuries were sustained. Because of the publicity the Battle Group is forced to try the NCOs in a special court. These are outstanding NCO's and no one in command wants to see their careers ruined. Your unofficial instructions. Lose the case."

I replied, "Lose the case? It's almost impossible to lose these cases, they don't go to court unless there is ironclad evidence."

He persisted, "Lose the case, Is that clear?"

"Yes sir. "

I departed, acquiring the case papers from the front office adjutant, and proceeded to find a way to lose. A week later, the trial began, and I successfully lost, and the NCOs were found not guilty. It wasn't too hard to lose. The officers sitting in judgment didn't want to find them guilty and were looking for any excuse to conclude with a 'Not Guilty' finding.

###

After the ruling, I met Major Badowski at the Infantry Bar. He was all smiles and bought me a beer. Later in the evening, he said, "I have another case for you. Your company commander will tell you to see me tomorrow morning."

On schedule, Captain Davies told me to report to headquarters for a special assignment. At Headquarters, I knocked on Major Badowski's door and he motioned me to come in. I reported,

"Lieutenant Damrill reporting for a special assignment."

The major responded, "I have another court-martial for you to try. This time you're going to win. I have all the evidence in this packet, but something that is not mentioned is missing.

It doesn't make sense, find the missing link?

Then he hands me the case.

"Yes Sir." I took the packet and left. Within one day of investigation, I found the link. I immediately went to see Major Badowski.

I knocked on the door and entered his office, "Sir, I've found the missing link. This case is tied to a group of 10 or 15 homosexuals on post. I know the names of two, but not the others."

This upset Major Badowsski and he said, "Damrill, there are no homosexuals in the Army."

"I know, but there they are, and I have drawings of the observed homosexual acts, provided by witnesses."

"Damn it, the bad publicity from this case would ruin the reputation of the Battle Group. You're off the case, give me your papers and evidence. If anyone asks you about the case, tell them you were excused from the case for a different, more important, duty assignment and I never had time to do any investigation."

"Yes Sir," I departed back to my company.

Looks like I'm finished as a trial counsel. Terrific.

The case disappeared and I was never informed further about the matter.

###

I met Major Badowski at the Infantry Bar, in the evening, and nothing more was said about my last case. Then later in the evening, he updated me on some future Battle Group requirements. He said,

"The Battle Group is to put together an honor guard company for a small ceremony in ten days. In attendance will be several United States senators, congressmen, and pentagon general officers visiting.

Captain Taylor, Commander, Company B is in charge, but his company can only field one of the two required platoons. He has requested that Company D provide the other platoon and that you be the platoon leader. Your company commander will tell you to report to Captain Taylor in the morning for detailed orders."

###

Captain Taylor had just been promoted and assigned as the Commander of Company B. He was a single West Point Officer, and we had been on several social outings with other single lieutenants. I had mentioned previously the importance of having facetime with your raters and their superiors. As a lieutenant, he was a master at modulating himself into high-profile positions. An example was when the division held an officer golf tournament. He volunteered for the committee organizing the event and made sure he was assigned highly visible authority tasks. He was responsible for organizing the first tee-off by Major General Train, Division Commander. He was responsible for the scoreboard and had the opportunity to review the player standings with all officers, which included his raters and post generals. Later, he was the person handing the trophies to the division commander, for presentation to the winners. When Major General Train supported a theatrical play at the officer's club as a fundraiser, the general played a lead role and the lieutenant volunteered to be a member of the group. His raters were also present at rehearsals, which allowed him to have social face-to-face encounters in a pleasant environment. The lieutenant used his off-duty time to the maximum for career advancement. He even dated Major General Train's daughter. Which could be a dangerous decision. I should have paid attention to his example because as soon as he was promoted to captain, he was given a command. Now he was to command the honor guard, to be viewed by United States Senators, Congressmen, and Pentagon Generals. After the ceremony, he was to join the party of dignitaries representing the junior commanders. Whether civilian or military, positive exposure to your bosses Is critical for advancement.

###

At our meeting, Captain Taylor reviewed the sequence of events for the ceremony. He said, "The event will take place on the main post at the end of a half-mile-long division parade field. At the end of the parade field were five general officer houses positioned in a semi-circle. At the base of the half-circle was a large World War I monument facing the parade field with the snow-topped mountain of Mount Rainier in the distance. The ceremony was to be short. The honor guard would already be in position with the division band playing as the dignitaries took their seats. There would be a few military commands, followed by the cannons firing a salute. The senators and congressmen would proceed to pin decorations on a few soldiers. At the conclusion, the honor guard would pass in review. Our first rehearsal is in two days. Get your platoons organized."

###

I reported back to Captain Davies of the mission and concluded, "Sir, to accomplish this task, I request the men in the platoon be my height for uniformity, and that they be under my command for the next ten days."

He's not happy about all my assigned special projects.

He reluctantly replied, "Okay Lieutenant Damrill, I hope this is your last task outside the company."

###

Everything went as planned with rehearsals. In between rehearsals, we got our rifles and uniforms in parade condition. The big day was slightly unusual for Washington, the sun was out, skies were blue and clear of clouds and Mount Rainier was majestic in the background. The short ceremony was spectacular.

###

That evening, I went to the Infantry Bar and sat down with Major Badowski. He said, "Congratulations on the parade. The officers of the honor guard have one more task. There is a division parade next week and you're to be escorts to guide the general and colonel's wives to their seats in the reviewing stand."

"That's great, but my company commander is getting testy about my additional assignments."

"Don't worry about it, he's an aviator or you might say glorified truck driver and doesn't understand," he said in a joking manner.

I wasn't sure what to say.

Line officers considered aviators as overpaid taxi drivers.

###

On the day of the division parade, I wasn't marching with my company, but at the division reviewing stand, escorting dignitaries. While performing my duties, Colonel Egan, the Division Artillery Commander's wife, and her daughter were standing there to be escorted. The daughter was home from a Colorado college for a few days before going back for graduation with a degree in chemistry. She looked interested, and we engaged in a short conversation before they were seated. We would meet again, in the summer, at the Officer's Club beach.

###

In the evening, I decided to go to the main officers' club, thinking that maybe the colonel, his wife, and daughter might be dining out. No luck in that category, but I found another adventure. It was the end of the month, and the finance office vault was full of money to pay the soldiers the next day. In the 1960s soldiers were paid in cash. The finance office was next to the officers' club. Someone decided to attempt to rob the finance office, and a shootout occurred. Bullets came through the windows of the bar, hitting bottles and some of the furniture. Fortunately, none of the patrons were hit. This could have been my adventure for the night, but I arrived ten minutes too late and again missed all the action.

###

A few days later, I ran into Major Badowski at the Infantry Bar, and we talked about the Battle Group going to Yakima for training in a few days. Towards the end of the evening, he said, "Captain Davies will inform you tomorrow morning to report to our Operations Officer (S-3), Major Black. Your assignment will be to train all the 81 mm and 106 recoilless rifle crews of the Battle Group while we are at Yakima Training Center. You will be cross training all the men, so they can do any task in their sections. They are to learn how to set up the mortars through crew drills, how to coordinate mortar firing in the fire control center (FDC), and act as forward observers to adjust mortar fire on the target.

"Well, I'm the weapon platoon leader of Company D, maybe Captain Davies won't object to this additional duty of training the other three weapons platoons in the Battle Group."

Did Major Badowski recommend to the S-3 that I be assigned this task?

CHAPTER 30.

In May 1961, the battle group left for Yakima Training Center, Washington. Everything was routine. After small unit tactical training, we had a three-day battle group exercise in Escape and Evasion. The purpose of this training is to practice how to escape when captured. After escaping, you evade the enemy by traveling during the night or periods of low visibility. After the exercise, we returned to Fort Lewis by motor convoy.

###

A couple of days after returning to Fort Lewis I went to the infantry bar where I ran into the Battle Group Executive Officer, Major Badowski. As part of our evening discussion he said, "The college Reserve Officer Training Cadets (ROTC) are to arrive in a couple of weeks. The battle group is to assist in their training. Our mission is to conduct the 106mm recoilless rifle block of instruction. The commander was impressed with your training of the recoilless rifles at Yakima. You'll be assigned this task shortly."

College ROTC cadets were required to attend a six-week camp between their junior and senior years. If successfully completed, they would continue to their senior year in ROTC and be commissioned upon graduation.

###

The next morning the Company Commander, Captain Davies, called me into his office and said,

"Lieutenant Damrill, go over to S-3 for an assignment. Headquarters wants you to instruct the ROTC cadets on the recoilless rifle."

I went over to the S-3 and reported, "Lieutenant Damrill reporting for assignment."

The S-3, Major Black responded, "You're to be the Officer in Charge (OIC) of the ROTC recoilless rifle training. Attached to you will be all eight recoilless rifles of our battle group. Another sixteen recoilless rifles will come from two other battle groups. You will present six, four-hour blocks of instruction over three days. Instruction will begin in two weeks. Everyone will assemble outside the S-3 tomorrow at 0900 (9:00 a.m.), at which time you will take command and start your rehearsals."

###

I went back to my company area and informed the company commander of my assignment. Following my report, he directed, "Go back over to headquarters the Adjutant wants to see you."

"Any idea what this is about?'"

"I'll let him tell you."

###

The Adjutant, Ed King is somewhat like the battle group commander's Secretary. In this case, he was a first lieutenant who was a Citadel graduate and had been with me in the Basics Infantry Course, the Berlin Brigade and now Fort Lewis.

I went over to headquarters and upon seeing the adjutant questioned, "What's the special occasion for the visit?"

He replied, "The division commander is looking for an aide and has requested the various commands each to send a representative from their unit for an interview tomorrow afternoon at 3:00 p.m. The commander has selected you to be his choice."

I've known him since we were commissioned. Was he the one who recommended me to the colonel?

###

The next afternoon, I was at the 4th Division Headquarters with nine other officers for the interview. The odds were one in nine of being selected. We entered the office of the Chief of Staff one at a time for a short interview. I didn't hear anything for a few days and thought I had lost out.

###

Two weeks later, at 8:00 a.m. I was about to start presenting my instruction to the ROTC cadets when I was called over to the field phone for a call from division headquarters.

"Lieutenant Damrill you were in the top three selected to be interviewed by the General for his Aide. He is going to interview at 10:00 a.m."

"Great! Wait, I'm about to start my block of instruction for the ROTC cadets in five minutes and will be committed for the next four hours. Can I come later?"

"Not sure if that's possible. I'll check and let you know."

The General interviewed at 10:00 a.m. and made his selection. I had forfeited my opportunity.

Being a general's aide would have been career-enhancing. I should have found a way to be there. This was another career mistake.

###

Summer of 1961, Fort Lewis had an outstanding officer's club system. You felt you belonged to an exclusive country club. Included was the officer beach club area on the Fort Lewis American Lake. It was laid out like a resort. Included, at the beach area was another club overlooking the water. It was built with logs and looked like it was constructed in the 1930s. Live music was heard, and waiters served refreshments on the beach. The military police (MPs) controlled the traffic. The beach was especially active on Saturday and Sunday as most stayed on post during the weekends since everyone worked till noon on Saturday. In the summertime, many of the colonel's and general's daughters came home from college for the summer break, with a few having just graduated. It was a wonderful place for them to hang out and a good place for single lieutenants to meet and talk to girls who were familiar with the military.

###

One afternoon, as soon as I arrived at the beach, I noticed the colonel's daughter who I had escorted to her seat at the recent division parade. Her father was the commander of division artillery. She had just graduated with a degree in chemistry. I walked over and introduced myself again, "I'm Lieutenant Damrill, remember I escorted you and your mom to your seats at the last division parade. Glad to see you again."

"That's right, I remember, it was a beautiful day, and the parade was fantastic. Let me introduce myself, I'm Pat Egan!'

"May I join you?"

Sure, wonderful idea, sit down."

We had an enjoyable time that afternoon. On following dates, we explored the northwest, which included the Cascade Mountains, Portland, Seattle, and the waterfront restaurants in Tacoma. However, at the end of the summer, she left for San Francisco to work for Gulf Oil. After she settled in at her new job, she sent me her address and telephone number. I would continue to see her from time to time.

###

It was great having an aviator as the company commander. As an aviator, he was required to fly four hours a month to retain his flying efficiency. One day, after we had passed all our inspections and tests, and reestablished company credibility, the company commander asked, "Lieutenant Damrill, I'm going for my four-hour monthly flight, do you want to go in the two-seat observation airplane, L-19?"

"Sure, when do we leave?"

I went along on several other flights. Usually, we flew over most of western Washington from the Canadian border to Portland, Oregon. From the air, you could see Mount Hood, Mount Rainer, and Mount Saint Helens. Mount Saint Helens erupted in May 1980, several years after my assignment in the area. On one occasion I noticed hundreds of WW II troop ships anchored in Puget Sound. I assume they were to be demolished and sold for scrap metal. Over Seattle, you could see them constructing the site for the 1962 World's Fair. At night, the lights were like watching a night light show. It was quite an adventure.

###

Near Fort Lewis was a VA medical facility located on American Lake. Student nurses were assigned there for a few months of practical training. They lived in the dorm on VA grounds that were isolated from the town. With the students away from their school and isolated, they were delighted to go out with single officers. I think it was an exciting activity for them to visit the various officer clubs. In the 60s these clubs were very active. The situation must have duplicated a wartime environment because several of the officers and students did get married after a short courtship.

I managed to become part of the group that frequented the officers' club, and I met a popular Japanese nursing student from Japan named Aiko Yamashita. I managed to get a date, and right away on the date, she explained her situation. "Ron, I am engaged, and my future husband is in the New York area studying to be a Neurosurgeon. With my knowledge as a nurse, I will be able to understand his position as a doctor. However, I was told I should go on dates with Americans and study the culture of the United States."

"Aiko, that's okay, neither of us will be at Fort Lewis very long."

She didn't tell me her family was the owner or one of the major investors in a large ocean shipping company. It may have been Mitsue O.S.K. Lines LTD, but I'm not sure. This is the company, that in April 2014 paid China a ransom of 29,000,000 dollars (2.92 billion yen) to get their ship, Baoseel from being hijacked. China declared this was owed to them from an old 1938 (China-Japanese War) debt.

###

It was fall, and several in the group decided to go to a University of Washington football game in Seattle and stay overnight.

I asked Aiko, "Would you like to go to the game."

"I hoped you would ask. I can arrange for my fellow students to stay with me at our attorney's family house in Seattle. They live on Lake Washington."

"Okay, we're on our way. The guys will stay at the Naval Station of Sand Point at their BOQ."

###

On the way to the game, the student nurses were dropped off at her family attorney's extravagant home. It was a very exclusive neighborhood with a guard at the front gate checking on arriving visitors.

We went inside and Aiko briefly introduced her student companions and their escorts as officers from Fort Lewis and named me as her date. The attorney, in his 50s, was cordial, but you could tell he wasn't overly excited that his daughter's client was going to the game with military officers.

He called me into the next room and explained with a stern face, "I assume you know who her family is. Make sure she gets back by midnight and don't become involved in any incidents.

"No, I really don't know who her family is. He looks worried. Did he have to approve Aiko's attendance at the football game? What type of incidents? Should I clarify what he meant? No, he doesn't want t to talk further.

"Yes Sir, we will have an uneventful time."

CHAPTER 31

The six of us arrived at the game 30 minutes before kickoff. I don't remember who the University of Washington (UW) played or the score, however, it was a great game. When leaving the football stands, we were separated from our group. Nevertheless, we continued down a small sidewalk path toward the parking lot, accompanying the crowd leaving the football game. While we were walking, I noticed a small hill to my right with what appeared to be a group of alumni in their mid-30s, still in party mode and not wanting the day's activities to end. As we approached them, I noticed they were staring in our direction, and as we got closer, they were glaring with disapproval. I could barely hear their grumbling, but I did hear the word Japanese. It was clear they were working up to a confrontation. Fortunately, I was able to maneuver Akiko deeper into the crowd that was moving quickly down the path, and we passed them before they could escalate. My guess is they were WW II veterans with Japan still vividly in their memories. An American collaborating with the enemy was treasonous. If the timing had been different, this could have developed into a small anti-Japanese confrontation.

I could see the headline in a Tokyo newspaper, 'Prominent Japanese family involved in an anti-Japanese brawl in the United States The U.S. nightly TV programs would carry a similar story.

Now, I understood what the attorney meant, when he said, "Don't become involved in an incident". I hope Aiko did not hear what the group was saying.

###

After the game, we went to several of the UW student after-game bars. Then we drove the nurses to the attorney's house.

###

The next morning, we picked the nurses up at 1200 hours and drove to Lake Washington where I had rented a motorboat. We looked for a beach to swim and lay in the sun. The weather was giving us a splendid day. Enroute, I decided to sit on the wet bow in a wet swimming suit. The boat was going about 10 mph when the driver decided to make a sharp right turn. The purpose was to see if I would slide off into the water. Of course, it was like I was sitting on ice, I slid into the water in a second. I could hear the boat passing overhead and I immediately opened my eyes. While underwater, I looked for the propeller. I watched it passing overhead, missing me by two feet. When I surfaced, Aiko exclaimed, "I was worried about the propeller."

"Me too, but it was a fun experience."

It was a lucky day, that this incident wasn't part of my own disaster. Since all was well, I joined in their laughter at my sudden swim. A month later, the nurses had finished their training and returned to their schools.

###

Back on base, the company commander was single and lived in the Fort Lewis bachelor officer quarters (BOQ). The BOQs for single commanders were much different than mine. His BOQ was located next to the general officer housing and was built in the 1930s. They were spacious and well-decorated. As my commander became well known, he began to have Saturday night social events in his quarters that I attended. At one of these social events, it was a quiet and rather boring evening with three lieutenants and their girlfriends attending, as well as my date and me. Suddenly the door opened, and there stood Captain Jim Ruff. I was surprised to see my previous company executive officer from Berlin. He and I always got into mischief. He had been reassigned to Fort Lewis, promoted to captain, and was a company commander in one of the other battle groups. Jim and I had many exciting adventures during our off-duty hours in Berlin.

###

Captain Ruff, as a commander, was living in the same bachelor officer quarters (BOQ) as my commander. He still looked like an 1890 boxer and had been on the boxing team at West Point and was a Russian linguist. He had heard the noise of our party and was checking it out. As soon as he saw me, he considered that he was invited. Usually, when there is a party going on in a BOQ everyone is invited. Not in this case, I noticed Captain Dunn, my company commander tensed up as if his space had been invaded. This meant there were two officers at his party with equal rank. I believe this situation was distressful for him.

Jim tended to drink too much. His language, when drinking, was sometimes boisterous and became a little aggressive, but he wasn't physically hostile. It wasn't long before Jim and my company commander soon developed a small verbal conflict. Jim likes good parties and is outgoing. Captain Dunn preferred a quiet sedate party with only select people invited. Captain Ruff hadn't been invited. Because I knew him, my commander told me to remove him from the party. He said, "He's your friend, I want you to tell him to leave, throw him out."

> *Remove him from the party? You're crazy, I'll be clobbered in ten seconds. Well, an order is an order, and he is my boss.*

I went over to where Captain Ruff was sitting and said in a low voice, "Jim, you have upset my company commander, and he wants you to leave."

Captain Ruff was shocked, "He what, Ron? I can't believe it! Have him come over and tell me himself. Anyway, I'm not ready to leave."

"Jim, I've been ordered to remove you from the party."

"Oh, go ahead."

After a few more exchanges, he was determined he would stay. I walked around behind his chair and tilted it up and he tumbled onto the floor with a thump. Then the tussle began. I knew he could easily put me in the hospital with a couple of quick punches. As we struggled, I was sure I was going to meet my demise, and that was when I had my first 'out-of-body' experience. There I was hovering next to the ceiling, watching the struggle below. Then suddenly, the thought came to me.

> *Wait, he is only half-hardily resisting, he's putting on a show. He knows my predicament and is letting me win.*

After letting me win, halfway down the hall, and out of listening distance, Jim stopped and said, "Good show, Ron. What's with Captain Dunn, sending a messenger to tell me to leave? It wasn't much of a party. I was getting ready to leave anyway."

I responded, "Thanks, for not clobbering me. I was surprised by the order. I should have quickly sidestepped it and made up some kind of excuse. It seemed the party was drifting along okay until another captain, you, came into his space. Then he became insecure."

Jim went on to explain his dismay at what happened, "Is this guy an infantry officer?"

I smiled and said, "He is an Army aviator, assigned one year to ground duty."

"Ron, I'm going over to the officers' club or to downtown Tacoma. Come with me."

"I'd like to, but I have a date that I have to take home."

I should have accompanied him, taking my date with us. Because, when you were with Jim Ruff, there was always an adventure around the corner.

It had been enough of a tussle that I had to buy a new suit. I was fortunate it was only the suit that was bruised. Overall, the outcome was a lucky night for me.

###

Jim continued his drinking adventures and eventually gained an unfavorable notoriety. Drinking in the 1960's was not a problem. However, the command encouraged troops to stay on post if they were going to drink. This would avoid negative publicity if you were off-post and unruly. If you were caught on post having one too many drinks it was not a big deal. Today, I understand if you get caught having too many drinks on the post it could be career-ending, sort of a reverse policy.

###

Jim had been able to handle drinks off-post in the past, however, he was starting to go over the line. He was in town with buddies, and they stayed until the establishment closed. After leaving, Jim remembered he had left his coat in the nightclub. He went back to get the coat. He could see people cleaning up inside and he knocked on the door. They didn't want to open. He persisted and crawled through a window. The employees then called the police. He was arrested, booked, and fined. Somehow, he survived command scrutiny and was still in command of his company. A couple of weeks later, his battle group was alerted to prepare for possible deployment to Germany. Captain Ruff was sent to Germany as a member of an advance party, to prepare the area for the battle group arrival. It was 1961 and Russia was building a wall dividing Berlin, which developed into the Berlin crisis.

###

The Berlin Wall construction started in August 1961, Creating an international crisis. Leading up to this event, Premier Khrushchev of the Soviet Union wanted all of Berlin to become part of East Germany. In November 1958, the Premier demanded that the West (France, Britain, U.S.) vacate Berlin in six months. However, in May 1959, the deadline was removed, and more negotiations continued. In May 1960, the Soviets shot down a United States U-2 spy plane over Russia, and diplomatic talks were suspended between President Eisenhower and

Premier Khrushchev. There was a United States election in the fall and Khrushchev counted on the new administration being more agreeable with his position. With President Kennedy's election, Khrushchev was hopeful that Kennedy would agree with him concerning Berlin.

###

Kennedy was hardly in office when the United States effort to support the invasion of Cuba failed miserably in May 1961. Kennedy had made changes to the Eisenhower plan and then major last-minute changes to the revised Central Intelligence Agency (CIA) Cuban invasion plans, that contributed to its failure. It was known as the Bay of Pigs.

###

In June 1961, Kennedy and Khrushchev met in Vienna to discuss Berlin. Again, Khrushchev didn't get the results he was seeking, regarding Berlin. Khrushchev was concerned because East Germans were fleeing to Berlin through many roads, canals, and trains at a rate of 1,500 to 2,290 per day. It is estimated that 3.7 to 4 million East Germans escaped to the West. Many of these were skilled refugees resulting in the East losing their professional base. As the wall was being constructed, the East German police and three divisions of military moved to seal off all arteries to and from the city. Kennedy made a public show ordering 148,000 National Guardsmen and Reservists to duty. One division of the 148,000 was sent to Fort Lewis.

###

Meanwhile, Captain Ruff was in Germany arranging the possible arrival of his unit. He and some other officers decided to visit the taverns in Germany during their free time. He did it again, he left his coat in a tavern that closed, and once more he demanded to be let in. The agitated German police were called. This incident came to the attention of the division commander who was less than impressed. Ultimately, my friend from Berlin was forced to resign. That was tough on him, he was anxious to see combat. Six months later officers were asked to volunteer for advisor duty in Vietnam.

Before resigning, he married an American Indian. I'm not sure how he and the 'firewater' worked out after he was married.

CHAPTER 32

Back in the company, I had my first, and last, experience as a banker. One of my private first class (PFC) soldiers had a financial crisis. He was married, and being new to the Army, his wife returned to live with her parents, to be near family support while she was pregnant. It was near the end of the month, and he had spent the small allowance he kept on hand. He sent most of his monthly pay to his wife. He came into my office with an embarrassed look on his face and asked, "Lieutenant, could you co-sign a loan for me for 200 dollars? My wife just had a baby, and I need to go home, but I'm broke and unable to buy a ticket."

He's really stressed.

In the 1960s there were no credit cards. If you needed money, you had to go to a bank and borrow it. The banks considered loaning to a PFC risky, they wouldn't loan the money unless he had a co-signer. I responded, "Congratulations, sure I'll help you out. I know your wife wants you home. Do you have the loan papers, or do we have to go to the bank?"

He passed me the paper, and I signed. I figured I had enough extra cash to pay off the loan if he defaulted. An hour later, the bank called to confirm that I had signed.

It didn't take long for the word to get around that I would co-sign a small loan. I must have signed ten more loans after that.

Everyone paid off their loan on time, that is, until the last one. There is always one person who takes advantage, he didn't pay, and of course I did. This concluded my co-signing adventure. The life lesson is never to loan money or co-sign a loan, especially to a friend, relative, or subordinate. If you do, there is a good chance the loan won't be repaid, and the loan will default. The co-signer is stuck having to pay back the borrowed money if he can. A friend indebted to you will most likely be resentful. If they need a co-signer, they can't afford the loan.

Today, banks have reversed their policy and offer you credit cards loaded with cash, hoping you will spend to the limit, and only be able to pay the interest. A large percentage of the population are slaves to the bank, paying only interest for the rest of their lives.

###

Six months have passed since I was assigned to Company D. Both the company and the 12th Battle Group were now operating efficiently. I went back to my routine of going to the Infantry Bar for my usual dinner of dill pickles on potato chips and I ran into the Battle Group Executive Officer, Major Badowski, again. In our conversation, he said, "The battle group commander and I are being transferred next week. We've done our job of getting the battle group backtrack. You've done a great job of helping 'straighten out' Company D, so now you're being transferred back to the S-3 shop."

How did he know about the order I was given by the previous battle group commander? "Damrill, straighten out Company D.

I should have asked, but I didn't know exactly what to say.

Finally, I said, "Sorry to see you go, we had a great time."

The Major replied, "I know, but it's time to see how the family is doing at Fort Bragg. See you around."

###

Company D heard of my transfer, and the day I was leaving, First Sergeant (E-8) Ford came into my office and invited me to have coffee in the mess hall. When we arrived, I noticed a table set up with a cake. The mess sergeant was standing by with a smile on his face. Seated at the table were the company's four platoon sergeants.

What's this?

Everyone stood up, as I walked in, then we sat down at the same time. This get-together was like a father-and-son meeting. All present NCOs were 5 to 15 years older than I and were combat veterans of either WW II, Korea, or both. We joked about my showmanship and finally Sergeant First Class (E-7) John L. Sullivan, Sergeant of the first Platoon went on to say, "We knew exactly what you and the battle group executive officer were doing, using recruit training drill instructor personalities. When we were finally convinced both of you were determined to follow through in improving the performance of the battle group, we joined in with our support. Thanks for the effort."

SFC Joe E. Lewis, Platoon Sergeant of the Third Platoon, went on to say, "We had almost given up. There were several years in a row that we had officers who sat around patting themselves on the back, bragging how great they were, doing little besides prancing around. Then we had a company commander relieved, and his executive officer was forced to resign for stealing money from the unit fund. The soldiers were aware of the poor leadership, and wondered what Army they were in."

SFC Jim Corbett, Platoon sergeant of the Second Platoon chimed in, "You made our job of disciplining easier. The soldiers decided it was simpler to do their jobs and conduct themselves like soldiers than go to the orderly room to be disciplined and listen to one of your 15-minute lectures while standing at attention."

SFC Rocky Marciano, Platoon Sergeant of the Weapons Platoon, nodded his head in approval and smiled.

This wasn't a meeting to tell me I was a superhero. It was more along the lines of telling me that I did everything possible to achieve positive results for a previously failing company. My NCOs had put me through a six-month initiation period, and I passed. I was okay.

Finally, First Sergeant Ford said, "We all appreciate you and the battle group executive officer, making sure that a not guilty verdict was needed in the special court-martial case against the two NCOs, that allegedly beat up a soldier. We were all watching and were curious if the officer corps was going to back up their NCOs.

How did they know? I was starting to get emotionally overwhelmed. It was getting hard to speak.

Fortunately, the meeting was over, and we all stood up and shook hands.

###

With the company having achieved high marks in all its graded areas of performance, they had previously failed, I was sure I would get an outstanding efficiency report.

###

Before signing into my old job in the S-3 as assistant operations officer, I decided to take a short leave to San Francisco. Before signing up for the leave, I called the colonel's daughter (Pat Egan), who I had met the previous summer, and who now worked for Gulf Oil in San Francisco, for a date.

I called her on a Monday evening, and when she answered, I said, "I'm taking leave and will be in San Francisco this Thursday night, will you be able to go out this weekend?"

There was a short pause, the dreaded pause, that sometimes comes before a rejection. Luckily, Pat replied, "That is a great idea. I'm anxious you see the Berkley campus. I'm doing some research there on Friday. How about meeting for lunch?"

I answered, "I'll be there". I proceeded to get the details as to the location.

###

I drove my Volkswagen bug to San Francisco. While driving up mountainous hills, with the Bug's small engine, I had to slow to 20 mph and shift to second gear.

This is an impressive car for a date with a future Gulf Oil executive. My Bug finally chugged its way to the Berkeley area. I checked into the BOQ at an army facility near the campus.

###

The next day, in October 1961, I drove through the entrance of Berkeley. I was astonished to see a booth, set up supporting Fidel Castro of Cuba! Castro had overthrown the government in Cuba in January 1959. He had immediately set up a communist government that was hostile to the United States. By March 1960, Castro had entered an alliance with the USSR, and later, Red China. The American public, and both political parties, demanded that President Eisenhower 'do something'.

###

The CIA developed a plan, and President Eisenhower approved. The plan proposed a covert action to infiltrate anti-guerilla Castro forces into Cuba. Recruitment and training would then begin within a month of plan approval. The unit became known as 'The Cuban Brigade'. The CIA immediately started building bases to support the operation. In the 1960s they built an airfield and training site at Retalhuleu, Guatemala in the Sierra Madre mountains near the Pacific Coast. There was also a staging base, "Happy Valley," at Puerto Cabezas on the Caribbean coast of Nicaragua, about 600 miles from Cuba.

Six hundred miles is a long way from Cuba.

The Anti-Castro Air Force consisted of about 16 Douglas B-26 Invaders, which were purchased from US Air Force surplus storage. This plane should not be confused with the Martin B-26 of WW II, obtained by Castro. The CIA had bought a different model aircraft than purchased by Cuba. The CIA B-26s were painted with Cuban colors in the hopes that they would be mistaken for Castro's aircraft. The CIA planners did not know, or paid little attention to, the fact the CIA's B-26s had a solid nose and looked nothing like the transparent nose of Castro's B 26s.

###

Elements of the Alabama Air National Guard were tasked with aircraft training and maintenance. They wore civilian clothes to cover their identity. US Special Forces were to train the ground forces.

###

Then 'mission creep' started. In other words, the mission was growing in scope beyond the original CIA plan. President Kennedy was sworn in on January 20, 1961. With Kennedy in office, the CIA changed its proposal from the program Eisenhower approved the year before. The original plan was to recruit, train, and infiltrate guerrilla forces into Cuba. The new plan, proposed to Kennedy, was an overt assault-type amphibious landing of 1,500 troops.

> My thought, *Invade Cuba, a country 780 miles long and 60 wide with just 1,500 soldiers? This plan was so bad, that the United States must have given a government contract to the Soviets to develop this strategy.*

Kennedy asked the Joint Chiefs of Staff (JCS) for their assessment of the plan. The JCS responded, "with complete surprise and complete air supremacy, with all of Castro's Air Force destroyed, the Brigade might last four days on the ground."

It would be impossible to keep the exiled community in Florida quiet about the venture.

###

As April 1961 approached, Kennedy started to have doubts and instead of calling it off, started scaling back in increments. The invasion was to go ashore at Trinidad in central Cuba, a hotbed of opposition to Castro. On short notice, the landing site was moved 100 miles west to the Bay of Pigs. The planners did not know it was Castro's favorite place, or that he was especially popular there.

You never make this kind of change at short notice. This is what happens when the CIA wants to be generals and play soldiers and when you have a junior senator who becomes President and is the top commander with no experience in Command or Organization.

Kennedy continued to micro-manage the operation. Two days before the landing, the exiled Air Force was to fly and destroy Castro's Air Force. On that day the Air Force was to destroy the Cuban Air Force, Kennedy decided that only six of the 16 B-26s should attack and to do only minimal damage. The Secretary of State, Dean Rusk, and Kennedy wanted the lowest US profile.

My thought was, *Was this equivalent to a sneak attack, like the attack on Pearl Harbor in 1941? The Japanese did attack displaying their country colors.*

Why didn't Kennedy want to ensure that all of Castro's Air Force would be destroyed?

###

These B-26s were only medium bombers and carried only a small number of bombs. With such a small number of aircraft in the attack, the Cuban Air Force wasn't destroyed. A second air strike was planned, but Kennedy canceled it. This left Castro with a small Air Force intact.

CHAPTER 33

The invasion of Cuba was launched just after midnight on April 17, 1961. This force of 1,500 invaders was opposing a 32,000 Cuban force. The CIA hoped for victory centered around the Cuban population rising in support of the invaders, which did not occur. Most of the population was not even aware of the attack. The CIA failed to find a way to notify the public of the invasion since they expected the population to revolt against Castro.

As they approached the shore, they were surprised to find the way to the beach was impeded by coral reefs. Therefore, the troops were offloaded 75 yards offshore. Analysts also predicted the beach would be deserted and quiet. However, it was lit up like Coney Island with a beach party in progress.

Was the invading force invited to the party and offered Rum Punch?

The beach, selected by Kennedy, was about four miles wide and 18 miles inland surrounded by a thick swamp with its only access by three gravel roads. The attacking force had surrounded itself with bad terrain. The Ivy League-educated civilian involvement in the planning and execution caused continuous confusion. Things were in disarray!

Changing the landing location at the last minute, without proper planning and reconnaissance, was foolhardy.

At dawn, the remaining Castro Air Force attacked the landing force and sank the resupply ships positioned offshore. The White House (micro-managing) belatedly authorized six B-26s close air support strikes for the ground force on the beachhead. Keep in mind that the airbases were 600 miles away. It took at least two hours from take-off to reach the combat area.

Close air support must be timely and responsive to the tactical needs of the troops on the ground. To have bombers wander over the battlefield, when it is politically convenient and dropping a few bombs is not helpful. I doubt if the troops even had ground-to-air communication.

These six B-26s took off at dawn on April 19. Four of the six B-26s were flown by pilots of the Alabama Air National Guard. When they arrived at the target area, they were met by T-33, American-made, jet fighters from the Castro Air Force. Two of the B-26s were shot down and crews were killed. Both planes shot down, were piloted by Americans from the Alabama Air National Guard.

The aircraft carrier USS Essex was offshore and authorized to provide 'very limited' air cover. The CIA, due to their inexperience in commanding a military unit, forgot to tell the Navy the time of the air strike. Fighters were still sitting on deck.

The invading force, out of ammunition and supplies (their supply ships sunk), surrendered on 20 April. About 100 had been killed, 360 wounded and 1,200 surrendered.

An inexperienced junior senator, who became President, taking personal command of an invading force, is like putting a second lieutenant in charge of the 1944 amphibious landing at Normandy. With our Harvard and Yale bureaucrats in charge of the government, the US continues to choose to lose. Our losses continue today under their guidance.

###

For a few days in April 1961, the US government kept up the pretense the failed invasion at the Bay of Pigs was the sole doing of the 'Cuban Patriots' seeking to overthrow Fidel Castro. However, it soon became clear that it had been planned and conducted by the Central Intelligence Agency (CIA) and that it was a complete disaster. The media blamed ex-President Eisenhower. As usual, this was purposely incorrect reporting by the media. Eisenhower planned to conduct an insurgent operation. Kennedy changed it to an invasion and later admitted it was his error.

###

The 1,200 captured prisoners were eventually released by Castro after he was given a ransom, from the United States, of five million dollars worth of food, and medicine. Many returned to the United States.

Several of the leaders were offered military commissions in the Army and Navy. A few years later, I had the opportunity to work with many of them. One day I was having lunch with one of the ex-commanders of the Cuban Brigade. We were of the same rank in the US Army.

During lunch, I asked, "What was the Bay of Pigs like?"

He responded, "It was a total catastrophe. The CIA told me, that the United States had an aircraft carrier nearby and that if I needed close air support, just call on the radio and help will be on the way. If you're successful in the invasion, you will be promoted to general."

I said, "I didn't know you received US close air support."

He continued, "We didn't. We were engaged in close fighting with Castro's forces and needed immediate close air support. I made the radio call to the carrier. No one answered, there was silence. We had been deserted on the battlefield by the CIA."

The halfhearted invasion was a failure. Castro remained in power and the USSR had a communist country ally just 90 miles offshore from the United States.

We're fighting communist expansion all over the world and yet we allow it to be established on our back door.

My visit to Berkley was in October, just six months after the 'Bay of Pigs'. I was amazed to see a booth on campus supporting an enemy of the United States. The students claimed it was their right to free speech.

We're fighting communist expansion around the world, but we support communism in the United States. This is strange and doesn't make sense to me.

To me, they were traitors. Where was our 'unity of Effort' to stand together in the face of the enemy? This activity, supporting the enemy of the United States on the Berkley campus was unbelievable and discouraging. That explained why the anti-Vietnam student campus riots began in Berkley. Students were supporting the enemy of the United States, with the encouragement of the faculty and California's politicians. They were cheering on the enemy to kill American soldiers. Pat, the colonel's daughter from Fort Lewis, was right, I needed to see the campus.

###

Pat and I had a terrific tour of the nightclubs on Friday and Saturday nights, with her friends. Sunday morning, I had some free time and decided to attend the Unitarian Universalist Church of Berkeley (UUIC). I expected the usual Sunday sermon. Not true, the church meeting was more like going to an anti-American political rally. My conclusion, the communists were established on the Berkley campus and the surrounding area.

This church was still a minority. However, there were numerous liberal ministers throughout the United States, such as William Chaffin, Jr., a Yale University chaplain, who went so far as to encourage civil disobedience.

###

After church, just to pass the time, I was sitting on an outdoor bench on the Berkeley campus. I thought no one was around and was reading out loud to myself some notes I had made and said the word communist. A young student seemed to appear from nowhere and was passing by he stopped, and said, "You know the word 'communist'. Is no longer used in the English language. It is tabu."

Before I could answer, he went on to say, "You should consider joining the DuBois Club of America. Here is an application, pencil, and stamped envelope. The post office box is over there. Make sure you mail it, I get extra credit from my Professors in Political Science, for every application they receive. Are you a professor?"

I responded, "No, I'm not a professor, just visiting the campus. Thanks for the information and application."

###

The DuBois Clubs of America was a national youth organization sponsored by the Communist Party USA (CPUSA). The organization was active in the American Student Movement of the 1960s and maintained a prominent presence on several college campuses including Columbia, University of New York, and California campuses such as Berkley.

Another popular communist club on the Berkeley campus was the Students for a Democratic Society (SDS) of which Tom Hayden was an activist. Hayden was the husband of movie star, Jane Fonda (Hanoi Jane).

I looked at my watch and it was time to pick up my date for swimming at Carmel Beach.

###

My adventures in San Francisco ended and I returned to Fort Lewis, Washington. I signed in at Battle Group Headquarters and then proceeded to my new job as the Assistant Operations Officer in the S-3. Arriving, I was surprised to see an unfamiliar captain in charge. I reported, "Sir, Lieutenant Damrill reporting."

I knew that the previous S-3 was departing and the new S-3, with the rank of major, was to be in position when I returned from my leave.

Who is the captain?

He could see the surprised look on my face and said, "I'm Captain Cooper, the temporary S-3. My assignment will be a 4.2-mortar platoon leader as soon as the new S-3 arrives. He has been delayed a couple of weeks. I'm glad you're back, we must get the training schedule out in three days. I understand you have done it before."

I replied, "Glad to meet you, Captain Cooper. The training schedule will be out on time."

###

One of my tasks in the S-3 office was to plan and print up the weekly training schedule. Printing up the schedule in 1962 was an interesting process. This method began two weeks before the training with the clerk typing up a training schedule for each of the six companies. Each schedule was typed on a stencil using a mechanical typewriter. If he made an error by striking the wrong key, he could correct a few errors with correction fluid, but the stencil was fragile and if too many errors were made, it would require starting all over with a new stencil. Our typist was a new Private First Class (PFC) with limited typing experience. As expected, many typing errors, and countless times were had to start over on a new stencil. Finally, the correctly typed stencil would be attached to a mimeograph machine to make paper prints. Our machines required you to manually feed the paper into the machine and then the operator would hand crank it to print. Upon completion, the pages were hand-correlated, stapled, and put into distribution. We finally received one technical breakthrough. It was an electric typewriter!

###

As the Assistant S-3, I served as the Forward Air Controller (FAC) for the Battle Group. After completing the training schedule publication, I requested to meet my driver of the FAC jeep.

When my driver came into my office, he reported, "SP-4 Damrill, your FAC jeep driver, you wanted to see me, Sir?"

We were both stunned, Damrill is a rare name, and we were probably the only two in the Northwest. After a short discussion, we decided we were cousins.

CHAPTER 34

The invasion of Cuba was launched just after midnight on April 17, 1961. This force of 1,500 invaders was opposing a 32,000 Cuban force. The CIA hoped for victory centered around the Cuban population rising in support of the invaders, which did not occur. Most of the population was not even aware of the attack. The CIA failed to find a way to notify the public of the invasion since they expected the population to revolt against Castro.

As they approached the shore, they were surprised to find the way to the beach was impeded by coral reefs. Therefore, the troops were offloaded 75 yards offshore. Analysts also predicted the beach would be deserted and quiet. However, it was lit up like Coney Island with a beach party in progress.

Was the invading force invited to the party and offered Rum Punch?

The beach, selected by Kennedy, was about four miles wide and 18 miles inland surrounded by a thick swamp with its only access by three gravel roads. The attacking force had surrounded itself with bad terrain. The Ivy League-educated civilian involvement in the planning and execution caused continuous confusion. Things were in disarray!

Changing the landing location at the last minute, without proper planning and reconnaissance, was foolhardy.

At dawn, the remaining Castro Air Force attacked the landing force and sank the resupply ships positioned offshore. The White House (micro-managing) belatedly authorized six B-26s close air support strikes for the ground force on the beachhead. Keep in mind that the airbases were 600 miles away. It took at least two hours from take-off to reach the combat area.

Close air support must be timely and responsive to the tactical needs of the troops on the ground. To have bombers wander over the battlefield, when it is politically convenient and dropping a few bombs is not helpful. I doubt if the troops even had ground-to-air communication.

These six B-26s took off at dawn on April 19. Four of the six B-26s were flown by pilots of the Alabama Air National Guard. When they arrived at the target area, they were met by T-33, American-made, jet fighters from the Castro Air Force. Two of the B-26s were shot down and crews were killed. Both planes shot down, were piloted by Americans from the Alabama Air National Guard.

The aircraft carrier USS Essex was offshore and authorized to provide 'very limited' air cover. The CIA, due to their inexperience in commanding a military unit, forgot to tell the Navy the time of the air strike. Fighters were still sitting on deck.

The invading force, out of ammunition and supplies (their supply ships sunk), surrendered on 20 April. About 100 had been killed, 360 wounded and 1,200 surrendered.

An inexperienced junior senator, who became President, taking personal command of an invading force, is like putting a second lieutenant in charge of the 1944 amphibious landing at Normandy. With our Harvard and Yale bureaucrats in charge of the government, the US continues to choose to lose. Our losses continue today under their guidance.

###

For a few days in April 1961, the US government kept up the pretense the failed invasion at the Bay of Pigs was the sole doing of the 'Cuban Patriots' seeking to overthrow Fidel Castro. However, it soon became clear that it had been planned and conducted by the Central Intelligence Agency (CIA) and that it was a complete disaster. The media blamed ex-President Eisenhower. As usual, this was purposely incorrect reporting by the media. Eisenhower planned to conduct an insurgent operation. Kennedy changed it to an invasion and later admitted it was his error.

###

The 1,200 captured prisoners were eventually released by Castro after he was given a ransom, from the United States, of five million dollars worth of food, and medicine. Many returned to the United States.

Several of the leaders were offered military commissions in the Army and Navy. A few years later, I had the opportunity to work with many of them. One day I was having lunch with one of the ex-commanders of the Cuban Brigade. We were of the same rank in the US Army.

During lunch, I asked, "What was the Bay of Pigs like?"

He responded, "It was a total catastrophe. The CIA told me, the United States had an aircraft carrier nearby and that if I need close air support, just call on the radio and help will be on the way. If you're successful in the invasion, you will be promoted to general."

I said, "I didn't know you received US close air support."

He continued, "We didn't. We were engaged in close fighting with Castro's forces and needed immediate close air support. I made the radio call to the carrier. No one answered, there was silence. We had been deserted on the battlefield by the CIA."

The halfhearted invasion was a failure. Castro remained in power and the USSR had a communist country ally just 90 miles offshore from the United States.

We're fighting communist expansion all over the world and yet we allow it to be established on our back door.

My visit to Berkley was in October, just six months after the 'Bay of Pigs'. I was amazed to see a booth on campus supporting an enemy of the United States. The students claimed it was their right to free speech.

> *We're fighting communist expansion around the world, but we support communism in the United States. This is strange and doesn't make sense to me.*

To me, they were traitors. Where was our 'unity of Effort' to stand together in the face of the enemy? This activity, supporting the enemy of the United States on the Berkley campus was unbelievable and discouraging. That explained why the anti-Vietnam student campus riots began in Berkley. Students were supporting the enemy of the United States, with the encouragement of the faculty and California's politicians. They were cheering on the enemy to kill American soldiers. Pat, the colonel's daughter from Fort Lewis, was right, I needed to see the campus.

###

Pat and I had a terrific tour of the nightclubs on Friday and Saturday nights, with her friends. Sunday morning, I had some free time and decided to attend the Unitarian Universalist Church of Berkeley (UUIC). I expected the usual Sunday sermon. Not true, the church meeting was more like going to an anti-American political rally. My conclusion, the communists were established on the Berkley campus and the surrounding area.

This church was still a minority. However, there were numerous liberal ministers throughout the United States, such as William Chaffin, Jr., a Yale University chaplain, who went so far as to encourage civil disobedience.

###

After church, just to pass the time, I was sitting on an outdoor bench on the Berkeley campus. I thought no one was around and was reading out loud to myself some notes I had made and said the word communist. A young student seemed to appear from nowhere and was passing by he stopped, and said, "You know the word 'communist'. Is no longer used in the English language. It is tabu."

Before I could answer, he went on to say, "You should consider joining the DuBois Club of America. Here is an application, pencil, and stamped envelope. The post office box is over there. Make sure you mail it, I get extra credit from my Professors in Political Science, for every application they receive. Are you a professor?"

I responded, "No, I'm not a professor, just visiting the campus. Thanks for the information and application."

###

The DuBois Clubs of America was a national youth organization sponsored by the Communist Party USA (CPUSA). The organization was active in the American Student Movement of the 1960s and maintained a prominent presence on several college campuses including Columbia, University of New York, and California campuses such as Berkley.

Another popular communist club on the Berkeley campus was the Students for a Democratic Society (SDS) of which Tom Hayden was an activist. Hayden was the husband of movie star, Jane Fonda (Hanoi Jane).

I looked at my watch and it was time to pick up my date for swimming at Carmel Beach.

###

My adventures in San Francisco ended and I returned to Fort Lewis, Washington. I signed in at Battle Group Headquarters and then proceeded to my new job as the Assistant Operations Officer in the S-3. Arriving, I was surprised to see an unfamiliar captain in charge. I reported, "Sir, Lieutenant Damrill reporting."

I knew that the previous S-3 was departing and the new S-3, with the rank of major, was to be in position when I returned from my leave.

Who is the captain?

He could see the surprised look on my face and said, "I'm Captain Cooper, the temporary S-3. My assignment will be a 4.2-mortar platoon leader as soon as the new S-3 arrives. He has been delayed a couple of weeks. I'm glad you're back, we must get the training schedule out in three days. I understand you have done it before."

I replied, "Glad to meet you, Captain Cooper. The training schedule will be out on time."

###

One of my tasks in the S-3 office was to plan and print up the weekly training schedule. Printing up the schedule in 1962 was an interesting process. This method began two weeks before the training with the clerk typing up a training schedule for each of the six companies. Each schedule was typed on a stencil using a mechanical typewriter. If he made an error by striking the wrong key, he could correct a few errors with correction fluid, but the stencil was fragile and if too many errors were made, it would require starting all over with a new stencil. Our typist was a new Private First Class (PFC) with limited typing experience. As expected, many typing errors, and countless times were had to start over on a new stencil. Finally, the correctly typed stencil would be attached to a mimeograph machine to make paper prints. Our machines required you to manually feed the paper into the machine and then the operator would hand crank it to print. Upon completion, the pages were hand-correlated, stapled, and put into distribution. We finally received one technical breakthrough. It was an electric typewriter!

###

As the Assistant S-3, I served as the Forward Air Controller (FAC) for the Battle Group. After completing the training schedule publication, I requested to meet my driver of the FAC jeep.

When my driver came into my office, he reported, "SP-4 Damrill, your FAC jeep driver, you wanted to see me, Sir?"

We were both stunned, Damrill is a rare name, and we were probably the only two in the Northwest. After a short discussion, we decided we were cousins.

–

CHAPTER 35

I immediately changed the exercise from a minor river crossing to an impressive amphibious landing on a beach at Fort Lewis. I put in a request for the training area on the beach and surrounding area for a follow-on tactical exercise. To transport troops to the dock, and to load the boats, I requested trucks from the division.

I can't believe it, no one is objecting to these requests or asking questions. Major McKeown (S-3) must have cleared the way and the division is interested.

I went to the post Public Affairs Office to coordinate news coverage. I walked into their office introduced myself to the lieutenant colonel in charge, and said, "The 12th Battle Group is conducting an amphibious exercise. Would you be able to contact the Tacoma, Seattle, and on-post newspapers, as well as local T.V. stations, to cover the exercise?"

He responded, "I've heard of the exercise at the weekly division staff briefing with the commanding general of the 4th Division."

Division weekly staff briefing discussing this exercise?

I continued, "Can you support our request? Do I need a written formal request?"

"No, we have it covered."

"Is it okay for me to talk directly with them, just before the exercise, to answer any questions they might have?"

"That would be fine; however, I want one of my public affairs officers present. My assistant will be eager to accompany you."

Additionally, I contacted our aviation unit and requested photos from the air of the exercise. The pilots were delighted with the task because it gave them practice with photoreconnaissance. Public affairs continued periodic follow-up visits with the news media. During this process, I also requested news cameras to cover the landing in the same manner as I had witnessed when I made an amphibious assault with the Marines at Camp Pendleton in 1952.

###

Two weeks into the planning I received a call from the MSGT Scott, "Lieutenant Damrill I've located a couple of cargo ships whose captains will let us use them for the exercise. The troops will board the ships and go over the side of the ship using cargo nets, just as it's done at sea. Of course, the ships will be docked the whole time. Do you agree, and can you locate a couple of cargo nets to put over the side of the ships?"

I responded with enthusiasm, "That's great, I'm impressed you could locate two ships. Yes, I know where two cargo nets are."

###

With all the details of the exercise completed, the S-3 wrote the Operation Orders for the exercise plan, directing in detail each commander and staff officer of their responsibilities. The plan also included convoy organization, the sequence for boarding the ship, and loading in the amphibious landing craft. And finally, the assault of simulated enemy positions after the beach landing.

###

The day before the exercise, accompanied by the assistant public affairs officer, we visited some of the nearby media and called those we couldn't visit. We reminded them of the exercise time, and location and answered their questions.

I also requested the assistant public affairs officer join me in visiting the Army Reserve unit supporting the operation.

###

On the day of the exercise, Colonel Wilson, Commander of the 12th Battle Group, took command of the convoy. To ensure an uninterrupted movement through traffic, to the Tacoma dock, he had a police escort. The motorcycle police were very impressive, with red lights flashing and blaring sirens piercing the air.

###

At the dock, there were newspaper cameras and T.V. crews everywhere. The soldiers offloaded from the trucks and boarded the freighters. They paused for pictures, then climbed down the cargo net into the amphibious assault landing craft. The amphibious reserve unit wasn't going to pass up publicizing their unit and cruised close to shore by numerous small cities and shore-side restaurants along Puget Sound. They paused briefly at each city and restaurant, so watchers onshore could take photographs. To ensure the amphibious craft were noticed, the U.S. Army Reserve Unit had the Harbor Police, waterfront firefighting boats, and Coast Guard escort them through Puget Sound with their light flashing. The firefighting boats created large fountains of water with their fire hoses. After a couple of hours of cruising, they arrived at Fort Lewis, at the designated time for the assault landing.

When the troops made their beach landing, they were greeted by the media, with many soldiers pulled aside for personal interviews. When the commander of the 12th Battle Group, Colonel Wilson waded ashore, he looked like General MacArthur, who waded ashore at the landing in the Philippines in October 1944, to liberate the Philippines from the Japanese. The exercise was a success and was covered on all the front pages.

###

With this media attention, the 12th Battle Group gained notoriety. This kept them in the headlines for a few more follow-up articles.

Colonel Wilson got his publicity for the 12th Battle Group. I am as pleased as he is. I'm not sure I'll ever be able to top this!

###

Back on base, the single lieutenant nurses got word that there were single Army infantry lieutenants from the 12th Battle Group attending Friday happy hour, at the hospital officers' club, and they decided to join in. The infantry officers had hoped for such an outcome.

###

In late 1961, Army doctors started prescribing a new diet pill to some of the housewives who had become slightly overweight and who were exhausted taking care of two and three young children. Besides losing weight, the pill gave the wives extra energy for their daily activities. To say the least, it was a popular diet pill and in great demand. The nurses noticed that it seemed to be more like a pep pill.

###

In the early 1960s, most officers were uninformed concerning recreational drugs. In the hospital, there were numerous samples of this 'diet pill' on shelves. One nurse, Lieutenant Sue Adams, gathered several of the samples put them in a quart jar, and brought them to happy hour so everyone could experience the energy of this pill. Sue handed them out by the handful. She came over to me and said, "Ron, take a handful of the pills. The drug representatives bring samples weekly. They're not a controlled drug."

Responding, I said, "Thanks, what is the strength, and how often can you take one?"

Sue responded, "Five milligrams and you can take one a day. I have an ample supply, take a handful."

Everyone thought they were approved, safe, diet pills with an added kick of energy. After a few weeks, the medical profession realized the pills had a form of SPEED in them. We chose this name to use in describing the pill. Distribution was quickly suspended, and I noticed the happy-hour parties were shorter in duration.

###

As the Battle Group gained success, the new commander, Colonel Wilson, on occasion, would join the single officers and nurses at happy hour on Fridays at the Madigan Army Hospital Officers Club. This made him a popular commander among the single officers. On one occasion, I mentioned to Colonel Wilson, "I missed all the combat action in the Korean War. It doesn't look like I will see combat anytime soon."

Colonel Wilson had been in both World War II and Korea. He smiled and said, "Don't worry, you will see more than you want."

Shortly after that, there was a call for volunteers for Vietnam in January 1962. Which began a 10-year-plus conflict.

###

As the assistant S-3, I was responsible for requesting and monitoring the status of the battle group training ammunition. Every quarter I receive a summary of the ammunition remaining in stock, for the remainder of the year. Reviewing the first quarter (October, November, and December), I noticed our allocation of 4.2 mortar training ammunition, identified only 50 percent remaining in inventory. We hadn't fired any 4.2 ammunition and 50 percent is shown as expended. These shells weigh 25 pounds each, which aren't easily transported if stolen.

We haven't used ammunition. Where did it go?

It wasn't unusual for someone in supply to be caught selling off military supplies or ammunition on the civilian market.

I went out to the front office where my driver was involved in some administrative tasks and said, "Specialist Roy get the jeep, we're going to the ammunition depot."

On the way to the depot, Roy asked, "Why the trip to the depot?'

I responded, "We're missing half of our 4.2 mortar ammunition from our battle group inventory. That's half of our original allocation for the year."

At the depot, I located the civilian in charge and showed him my quarterly report. I pointed to the 50 percent figure and said, "We haven't used any of this 4.2 ammunition, where is the other 50 percent?"

He was slightly embarrassed, and his face turned red. He said, "I was ordered to issue it to another unit."

Responding, "Which unit, and who ordered the transfer?"

He answered, "I'm not sure who at post headquarters ordered the transfer, I just did what my boss said."

I returned to the battle group and reported the ammunition shortage and my discussion with the civilian at the depot, to the S-3, Major McKeown who said, "That's a surprise, I'll look into it."

The next day the S-3 called me into his office and said, "I found out about the ammunition. You can forget about it and don't ask, it's too complicated to explain."

This comment usually means something irregular happened.

I thought there would be a strong response to our lost ammunition. This was a good teaching lesson for me. A commander, such as Colonel Wilson, is only in command for a short time. He doesn't want to be distracted by minor disputes over an issue that will probably resolve itself over time.

###

A few of the officers decided to start going to Mount Hood in Oregon for snow skiing. This was a four-hour drive. The attraction of Mount Hood was that they had accommodations for staying overnight. Supporting the lodge, were numerous nightclubs offering music and dancing for the skiers after a day of skiing. One December morning, close to Christmas, I remember having a coffee on the second floor and looking down on all the activity in the lobby and wondering,

Where will I be next Christmas?

That evening I saw, what looked like a blond Swedish girl, sitting with a group of girlfriends in one of the skiers' nightclubs. I walked over and introduced myself, "Hi, I'm Ron and I live near Tacoma, Washington, are you local?"

She responds, "Well, Ron I'm Sonia, my friends and I are students at Pacific Lutheran University."

"You're kidding, I live just two miles from your campus."

She went on to say, "My hometown Is Portland. Just so you know, my father is the police chief there."

We both laughed and then she said, "It's true, he is the police chief."

I responded, "You have an interesting dad, I'll bet he has some fascinating stories."

Sonia said, "You aren't concerned about socializing with a police chief's daughter. In that case, invite your friends to join us."

Looking over at my friends, "They must have heard your invitation, I see they're almost here."

Later in the evening, she agreed to go on a date the following weekend in Tacoma. We had a couple of dates and became good friends. One weekend we went skiing together. After a downhill run, it was clear she was a much better skier than me. My inability to keep up with her proved to be my undoing. She was an excellent skier and my only interest in skiing was just to be in the mountains. There aren't many hills in Kansas. However, we remained friends.

###

CHAPTER 36

In January 1962, I was promoted to captain. It had only been four and one-half years since my commissioning. It was also my 29th birthday. Things were moving along at a rapid pace. When promoted in the army you're expected to give a promotion party.

How can I make this different from other promotion parties?

The 12th Battle Group had just received several new single Second Lieutenants, who had aa graduated from college the previous summer and had just completed the Infantry Basic Officer Course at Fort Benning, Georgia. They were still in the process of adjusting to Army life.

I have an idea I'll ask Sonja to come to the party and bring several of her sorority sisters.

I put the plan into action and called Sonja, "I'm having a promotion party a week from this Saturday at the Fort Lewis Officer Club. Attending will be several new single Second Lieutenants. Can you come and bring some of your sorority sisters? After the party, we'll all go to the McChord Air Force Officers Club, next to Fort Lewis. It's always packed on the weekends with a fantastic dance band."

There was a pause, then she said, in an excited voice, "I'll see who's available."

Four days later Sonja called, "Ron, I'll be able to come to the promotion party and I'll bring four girls with me."

I responded, "That's great, I'll see you there."

The party went as scheduled, with a band, hors d'oeuvres and drinks. All the officers in the 12th Battle Group were there. Married officers attended with their wives. Sonja showed up with her friends and they were the best-looking girls I had seen since my arrival at Fort Lewis. They were so attractive that the new single Second Lieutenants were too shy to talk to them. Finally, the girls went over and introduced themselves. Then one of the girls said to one of the officers, "Would you like to dance?"

The second lieutenants loosened up and they all began to socialize.

Afterward, the single officers and girls went to the Air Force Officer's Club and danced to the "Twist."

###

I shouldn't mention all these encounters. But, having come from a small town in Kansas it was quite an experience meeting all these interesting people. Even for a short period.

###

In 1961 the conflict in Vietnam, between the North and South was becoming more intense. Vietnam was viewed as just one front in the emerging global battle of Capitalism Democracy and Communism, with Communism on the march. China had fallen in 1949, North Korea had invaded South Korea in 1950 with the backing of Stalin, and in January 1951 China sent troops to assist the North Koreans. In 1954, Vietnam, supplied with weapons from China and Russia, defeated the French. Vietnam was divided into North and South by peace agreements. The North is aligned with China and Russia and the South is aligned with the West.

###

In the Spring of 1954, President Eisenhower described what he believed was at stake for the West and Vietnam and coined the phrase, 'The Domino Theory'. This theory was that if one country fell to communism, then maybe a neighboring country would fall to communism. Like dominos, they would fall one after the other, and South Vietnam was seen as the next domino to fall.

###

In the Vietnamese struggle, to overthrow the French in the 1940s and 1950s, separate political factions developed, but then united to fight the French. However, as soon as victory had been achieved in the North, Ho Chi Minh, a Soviet-style Communist gathered up the leaders of the various factions for a meeting and then had them all killed, leaving Ho Chi Minh in charge of the North. As background, Ho Chi Minh was born in 1890, and at age 21 left Vietnam to travel to New York, London, and France. In France, he joined the Socialist Party. Later he went to Russia and joined the Communist International, an organization tasked with spreading communism throughout the world. Then he went to China in the late 1930s, as a Russian' representative to set up both the Chinese and Vietnamese communist Parties. In 1941, after 30 years he returned to Vietnam as, a devoted Stalin communist whose purpose was to lead a guerilla uprising to overthrow French colonialism.

###

In the mid-1950s Ho Chi Minh began supporting an irregular army in the South in violation of the 1954 Agreement. President Eisenhower didn't want South Vietnam to be another domino to fall to communism. However, he didn't want to commit United States ground forces. Instead, he sent economic and military aid, and 900 "advisors" by 1959.

###

Also, in July 1959, Castro took over Cuba.

The Domino Theory? Ciuba fell to communism. The United States was next to Cuba. Would the United States fall to communism?

###

President Kennedy became president in January 1961 and increased the "advisors" to 3,200 in his first year. In late 1961 he decided that military "advisors" should extend down to the battalion level. The rank of these new battalion "advisors" was captain.

###

In January 1962, Captain Joe Hicks, a friend who had been promoted with me, came into my office and said, "They are looking for volunteers to go to Vietnam as battalion advisors. Let's sign up!"

I responded, "No kidding, the adjutant should know. Let's go over to his office and see if he has any information."

The adjutant, Captain Ed King had also recently been promoted. He and I had been in the same organization since we were commissioned.

###

The adjutant was at his desk, and we asked if he had heard about volunteering for Vietnam. He said, "It's true, I've just signed up, and here are the forms."

We excitedly took the forms and quickly filled them out and gave them back. Captain Hicks and I returned to the S-3 section and my boss, the S-3, Major McKeown, motioned us to come into his office. He said, "I've got some great news for you, they're asking for volunteers for Vietnam."

He noticed we weren't surprised and said, "I thought both of you would be more enthusiastic."

We smiled and I said, "We just signed up."

The major was disappointed he didn't break the news first.

Then Captain Hicks asked the unthinkable question, "Where is Vietnam?"

I responded, "I don't know."

Major McKeown got a smile on his face and said, "There is a world globe in the corner, and I have pasted a star on the Vietnam location."

###

After volunteering we then waited to see if we were accepted, and if accepted, how soon would we depart Fort Lewis? Feeling sure we would, Captain Hicks commented, "Let's go to Mount Hood, Oregon this weekend for one last time skiing on the snow before going to the tropics."

"Great idea, let's get a weekend pass so we can leave Friday night."

We arrived about 9:00 P.M. on Friday and we immediately went to a popular nightclub that was already packed. Looking for a place to sit, we noticed two empty stools at the bar. Sitting alone, next to one of the empty stools was a 26-year-old girl who could have been Miss America or Miss Universe.

How could a girl that attractive be sitting alone? Were guys afraid to talk to her?

As I approached the seat next to her, I noticed she was drinking a plain Coca-Cola. Sitting down I said, "Hi, I'm Ron, mind if I sit next to you?"

She responded, "I'm Tess Monroe from Portland, Oregon and just arrived. I used to come here often. Do you want to dance to the tune they're playing? It's one of my favorite songs."

I think girls always want to get on the dance floor, to be better seen.

"Great idea, Tess."

This was one of those rare times when personalities were instantaneously compatible. I couldn't believe it. During our conversation, she said, "Ron, I just signed my divorce papers today, and I thought I would celebrate by going skiing alone. I should tell you I have a three-year-old boy and have temporarily moved home with my mother."

Responding, "Okay, nothing serious, we'll just have a good time."

This was my first encounter with a divorcee' and was a different adventure. We met several times for skiing and dinner. On Sunday we departed, and Tess agreed to a date the following week. I was to pick her up at her home in Portland.

###

On the following Tuesday, I received orders for South Vietnam. I had about three weeks left at Fort Lewis. Before going to Vietnam, I was to attend a one-month orientation course, Military Assistant Training Advisors (MATA) at Fort Bragg, North Carolina. Just my luck, I met an outstanding girl, just before being transferred.

###

The weekend arrived and I was off to my date in Portland with Tess. Following my map, I ended up in an exclusive gated neighborhood. The guard stopped me and wanted my identification. He checked it against his list of expected visitors, provided by the homeowners.

Am I on his list?

The guard saw I was a little nervous and slowly looked through his papers with a serious look on his face. Finally, with a smile, he said, "Continue to the address on the pass."

With my economic VW bug, I put through the gate past numerous luxury cars such as Cadillacs and Mercedes. The designated address was a beautiful, small mansion. I rang the doorbell and Tess's mother opened the door and said, "We've been expecting you. Tess will be down in a few minutes."

"Thank you, you have a beautifully decorated house."

There was small talk for a few minutes and her mother finally said in a very cordial and subtle manner, "I encourage Tess to go out, but I don't want her to become serious with a nomad military officer. I expect her to stay here in Portland."

Responding, "I understand, we'll keep it on a friendly basis."

I didn't tell her I was on orders and leaving Fort Lewis shortly.

Tess and I went on a few more dates in the Portland area and had a magnificent time. But the acquaintance was too short to carry over into the future.

It looks like, if you find someone you like you better ask them to get married on the first date.

###

With our orders in hand, Captain Hicks approached me and asked, "Would you like to go to Mardi Gras with me. It will be starting about the time we arrive, and I have a friend, with an apartment on Bourbon Street in New Orleans, and were invited to stay with him."

"That's an outstanding invitation. Sure, I'll go."

He said, "There will be three of us traveling in my car. One of the single nurses we know from Madigan Army Hospital, Lieutenant Sue Addams. The girl who had the diet pills at happy hour wants a ride to Louisiana."

"I remember her, she will make great company."

###

I sold my VW Bug and then downsized my remaining possessions to one duffle bag. I had been assigned to Fort Lewis for 18 months and had four separate assignments, working for four different bosses (ratters), four different endorsers, and three battle group commanders. A rater provides one-half of your evaluation and the endorser the other one-half. I worked for eight supervisors in 18 months. Now this is what I call a stable lifestyle.

###

Made in the USA
Columbia, SC
04 November 2024

45408578R00153